university college
for the creative arts
at canterbury, epsom, farnham
maidstone and rochester

Rochester, Fort Pitt, Rochester, Kent ME1 1DZ 01634 888734
This book is to be returned on or before the last date stamped below.
Fines will be charged on overdue books.

Decio Giulio Riccardo Carugati

WALLY

Electa

cover
Esense
photo Gilles Martin-Raget

texts
Jason Holtom, Monica Paolazzi

graphic design
Andrea Fanti, Guido Grugnola
Industrial&Corporate Profiles, Milano

page layout
Industrial&Corporate Profiles, Milano

editorial coordination
Monica Paolazzi

editing
Simona Oreglia

technical coordination
Mario Farè

quality control
Giancarlo Berti

translation
David Smith

photography
Gilles Martin-Raget

Carlo Borlenghi
Robert Bösch
Guido Cantini
Guy Gurney
Anthony Holder
Industrial&Corporate Profiles
Kos
Nico Martinez
Toni Meneguzzo
Franco Pace
Matteo Piazza
Philip Plisson
Neil Rabinowitz

typography
wallytype

The publisher wishes to thank Wally
for kindly providing the photographs
and the texts for this volume

www.wally.com
www.electaweb.com

Wally came into being, was inspired by and evolved around three great passions: passion for the sea, passion for technology and passion for beauty. Right from the first boat Wally has tried to satisfy these passions in the most absolute way possible, rejecting all compromises.

A sort of Free Flight into a man's dreams.

All the people who have taken part in this Free Flight, collaborators and customers, have dreamt, have endured and have enjoyed this challenge against everything and everyone.

We tackled the laws of physics and mechanics, we fought our competitors in the market place and on the race course, we struggled against our friends' mistrust, but in the end we won.

Today we feel we deserve what we have achieved. Wally does not only mean sailing faster and in greater comfort. Wally also and above all means being courageous, pitching your heart beyond the obstacle and feeling free, precisely due to this ability to get away from stereotypes.

Without seeking it, Wally has perhaps become a way of thinking and living.

Fifteen years after the first "Wally idea," this is the definition that gives me the greatest satisfaction and further motivation to continue, trying to apply this way of thinking to other products and other moments of life.

I thank my mother and father for teaching me how to be "Wally."

Luca Bassani Antivari

Looking at the word "design" in its twofold function of noun and verb, the respective meanings include: intention, purpose, plan, intent, aim; to organise, to act strategically. And Vilem Flusser, in *A Philosophy of Design*, comments: "It isn't a question of understanding from a historical viewpoint, that is, in the sense of having to seek out facts that would demonstrate where and when the word took on its current meaning. It is a question of a semantic nature in the sense that the aim is to elicit reflection on why the word has assumed this meaning in the contemporary debate."

Intention is very fitting when, in the Wally case, design distinguishes the excellence of design-related ethics aimed at improvement of the object boat, in all its performance values. An intention which becomes action, strategic plan, special and exclusive behaviour.

This is how Industrial & Corporate Profiles' exceptional graphic design, the fine images, bear witness to the harmonious development of Wally style. Similarly the text by Jason Holtom provides a valuable counterpoint to the iconographic vision. I conducted the interview with Luca Bassani.

My thanks to Monica Paolazzi for her invaluable contribution in defining the plan of the work. Thanks also go to Virginia Ponciroli, Simona Oreglia, Giancarlo Berti, Paolo Verri and, in the persons of Stefano Peccatori and Luciano Mornacchi, the whole Electa editorial staff.

Decio Giulio Riccardo Carugati

"Owning a Wally is not just being part of an exclusive club, it is having the feeling that you are actively participating in building the brand —some would say the myth—itself. As a lover of motor sport and its history, I am struck by the similarity with the beginnings in the early 1950s of another great Italian brand: Ferrari."

Sir Lindsay Owen-Jones

"The first rule when deciding to conceive and build your new superyacht is to dream and try to make your

dream become real. Is there anything better than making your dreams come true?"   Luca Bassani Antivari

A Clearly Indentifiable Plan

An Interview with Luca Bassani

"The continual seeking of difference is an integral part of the evolutionary mechanism ... The luxury of the future...," notes Hans Magnus Enzensberger, "will in all probability be available only to a small minority ... No duty-free-shop can offer what really counts in life: time, attention, space, tranquillity, environment, security..." Among these, the German poet-philosopher points out, "...time is the most important kind of luxury ... a life of luxury is lived by those who have always have time available solely for what interests them, who can decide how to occupy their time, who can decide not only what to do but where and when to do it..." If time is the most important kind of luxury, where and how can this small minority experience the privilege they have acquired? Among the few lucky ones who are also sophisticated yachtsmen there is no doubt: the boat is the where and the how, the place and the way to best exercise exclusive behaviour.

Luca Bassani says: "That's it, a boat is the top luxury item. I can't see any others. If on a technical level it is used for the transport of people and goods, while under way it allows you to enjoy spaces and services, it is the only means that brings you into and makes you a part of the natural landscape. Whereas even the most comfortable plane is nothing more than a shuttle from one airport to another, just as the train takes you from one station to another and your car from one motorway pay-toll to another. So a boat gives you the most freedom of all. Although, and I am talking about cruising sailboats, there is usually a lack of that private luxury which is made up of attention to all performance values. Pleasure sailing has a very recent history. Until the early 20th century sailing had military or fishing connotations, or had to do with the transport of goods or passengers. No one yet went to sea just to enjoy it. In fact those who did so in times now remote called themselves explorers. So yachting is a very fresh culture with little tradition. It would reach early maturity in the 1960s with the definition of different models. And it was here that sailboats, slower than powered craft, were built to stand up to bad weather rather than for the enjoyment of the sea. Actually the phenomenon lasted for only 5 per cent of a season, while for the rest of the time the boat was uncomfortable, closed and useful only in emergencies. The Genoese, great sailors, say 'u ma,' meaning the sea, but also meaning evil, fear of the sea. This wise admonition certainly

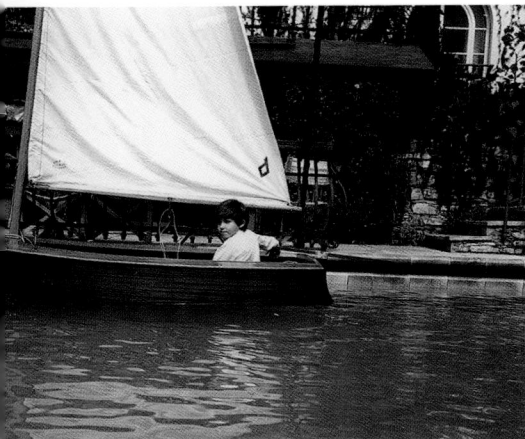

cannot prevent enjoyment of the sea. In fact to these ends people who had no enthusiasm for sailboats chose the equivalent of the car—the powerboat. It isn't by chance that Carlo Riva's Aristons and Aquaramas are built on the lake and immediately turn up in Portofino, Saint Tropez and Monte Carlo. They're easy to handle. For a day of sun and sea just offshore, you don't have to hoist a sail but simply switch on the ignition. Likewise for a swift return to port at the first sign of a change in the weather. I've been a racing

and cruising yachtsman for about forty years. Nowadays we take it for granted that they'll tell us if the weather will be fine or nasty tomorrow. This wasn't the case as recently as fifteen or so years ago. And even less so when I started racing. I remember as an adolescent my maths teacher at high school was an air-force colonel, a meteorologist at Linate Airport. I pestered him with questions and he courteously gave me explanations. It got to the point that on

Fridays, when he knew I'd be racing on Saturday and Sunday, he would kindly bring me the forecast for the weekend. I'm still grateful to him today. Sailboat cruising has evolved less than motorboat cruising. It was and is a niche market formed by a few keen enthusiasts. In the 1960s and 1970s the leader was Sparkman & Stephens. Olin Stephens was the designer while his brother Rod, an expert sailor, experimented with the models at sea, suggesting modifications and fine tuning. At that time the only comfortable sailing yachts were the great and glorious 30 to 40 metre vessels of the 1930s, but they required large crews and costs were prohibitive. Only in the late 1970s-early 1980s did the first roller furling jib and mainsail handling systems appear. This meant a considerable reduction in crew. My father, who intended to withdraw into private life at the age of sixty, had decided two years earlier in 1978 to make himself a present of a new 'retirement' boat. My brother and I had a hard time but in the end we got round to convincing him: instead of a motorboat, a 30-metre sloop, my first design and the last boat built by Camper & Nicholson before the famous shipyard was refounded. Moreover it was the first yacht of its size built in the second half of the last century. It had roller furling main, jib and staysail, a considerable innovation in those days. So a new, more comfortable generation of big yachts came into being, but the running rigging, apart from the three sails mentioned above, still had to be handled manually. So guests had to keep well

"Our goal is to spread through images the strength and the beauty of our products."

sheltered in the cockpit while sheets flew around and cracked like whips. At that time a 43 footer was considered average size, a 55 was already big and the 95 was a size wholly unexplored. Today an average size yacht goes from 24 to 30 metres. Anything less is considered small and the big ones start at 40 metres. So until the 1990s there was no real evolutionary impetus. Though aluminium had replaced wood as a building material, from the viewpoint of configuration of hull and mast all cruising sailboats looked the same, their forms absolutely traditional. No designer would dare to suggest anything different when the sole reference point was racing boats and the racing rules conditioned their definition. So they weren't the fastest overall but rather the fastest within the limits imposed by the rules. Nobody would dare to stand outside those schemes that were considered unalterable. It should also be said that the little research carried out—in test tanks for example— concerned only the America's Cup. Designers created the positive and negative, racing hull was conceived as absolutely empty and therefore light, fast and manoeuvrable, whereas a cruising yacht was encumbered by equipment for housing guests and things, furnishings and whatnot. I thought of looking into those technologies that would allow me to create an even lighter hull in order to gain that margin needed for the cruising set-up, carpentry, systems etc. My research was immediately oriented towards a new possibility: carbon for both hull and mast. Though the best known designers

established what was good or bad, safe or unsafe. In 1989, when I decided to build the first Wally boat, the first Wallygator, the situation was still that way. Although the rules were changing: racing boats began to appear with wide sterns, high freeboards and considerable volume while cruising boats were still obstinately built as thin as cigars with a very narrow stern, understandably uncomfortable inside and out, and also slow. A really intolerable contradiction. I said to myself that I'd have to succeed in making a cruising yacht out of a racing yacht. In a word, by turning everything inside out. And I thought about how the

"Our typical client culturally loves challenges and is not bound by stereotypes that tie him down to tradition."

assured me of satisfactory tests in a racing context, none of them was willing to experiment with the Wally concept. But I was determined to have a hull and mast in carbon. The structure being stronger, it would solve my sail plan problem. In fact what I wanted was a mainsail and a small self-tacking jib. Against all opinions I was convinced that you didn't need a huge genoa to make a big boat shift along. Everything was clear in my mind. I had designed it, sketched details and some views of its general development. What I lacked was a

performances, comfort, safety and speed. The latter was primary (more speed = more fun), but the others equally so. It's not a play on words. I mean when comfort is understood as liveability on deck and below, ease of manoeuvring, and safety as a deck free of dangers both underway and at anchor. Running rigging concentrated in specific zones separate from the socialising areas. The boat, plaything par excellence, with the use of technological automation and the

relationship with a good marine architect willing to take a risk. That's when I developed an understanding with Luca Brenta. In the years that followed we worked with many other people. He had already designed boats such as Marisa which, big and beamy, was a really fast racer. These features corresponded very well to what I was after in my design. So Wallygator came into being. I had solved more than a few problems: from research to application of advanced technologies and the achievement of closely correlated

most advanced building materials, creates a harmonious conciliation of the functions represented: the exclusive spectacle of a manoeuvre carried out which applauds and satisfies the crew as much as it satisfies those who, out of the shade of the sails, lying in the sun, wholly relaxed, without fear and secure, admire the multiple effects of the dynamics, fascinated by a representation of the compatibility of presumed opposites: the high performance of the boat and the high level of comfort on board. Exclusive design, luxury, true luxury. I still remember with feeling the time when I was rowing ashore in the launch, having dropped anchor at

Portofino, and Wallygator seemed to me, beyond the shadow of a doubt, the most beautiful boat of all. And she really was, with her achieved synthesis and innovative design. Today the vertical bow and the single colour hull are seen as Wally stylistic features, and all racing boats use a small foresail instead of a big genoa. And who other than Wally had adopted it almost twenty years back for cruising yachts? They all now have masts with swept back spreaders, which our first mast in carbon already had. The shrouds are

convinced that the best way is to consider every item produced as a step along the way, a workshop, a mine of ideas for constant confirmation of the Wally system and strategy. Our background can be summed up in the fact that we have always been one step ahead of the others. And in this sense we defend the uniqueness of Wally products. We try to make increasingly faster and more comfortable boats.

set at a wider angle, reducing the force exerted. In the 1992 America's Cup Il Moro di Venezia experimented with a carbon sail fabric that turned out to have structural defects and, among other things, it fell apart. In 1994 with the second Wallygator, a two-masted ketch, we perfected performance with a sandwich system: very light cloth as a support for the carbon, holding together the load-bearing fibres. We immediately produced a jib that gave surprising results. All the latest generation of large boats now carry similar sails. I've often wondered how to vindicate these intuitions. And I'm

A challenge in which we are aided by certain owners: an even more exclusive niche that joins and identifies with our way of doing things, with the terms of our constant evolution. We tackled the powerboat, considering speed as a function of reducing travelling time because, unlike under sail, there's no fun or pleasure in just moving along. If statistics assign 30 per cent to a flat calm, 50 to a choppy sea and the other 20 to a rough sea, our motorboats stand out for being fast in up to 60 per cent of the conditions. That's already an extraordinary result, and it's due to the special design of the hull. WallyPower is exemplary, where the design criterion is still the same, aimed at the broadest performance result: comfort, speed and safety. Commitment is our strength, our heritage, our culture. Of course copies of our details, our most innovative solutions, are inevitable, but in other people's productions they look false, unjustified, removed from a general context. Our way of doing things has now become a trademark guaranteeing integral design, where each individual detail contributes to the excellence of the whole. In this sense our work is aimed at the achievement of

outstanding models, and these more than anything else mark an end of unexciting traditional designs. If it is true that everything has already been done, everything can be done again, better. And in fact, paraphrasing the Buddha's words 'It's better to travel well than to arrive,' we never consider the adventure, the design experience, as being over. In confirmation of this we're looking into a new idea: a vessel whose conception is such that it could be built at low cost

"I always saw Wally as a luxury brand, not just a shipyard."

shipyards. I'm thinking about China. A freighter, a small tanker. The WallyIsland idea grew out of a reflection: the costs of a vessel is worked out from its volume, so why build it vertically with a castle of decks? With horizontal development what you get first of all is a far more seaworthy craft, longer on the waterline, better looking and more practical. Formerly unimaginable possibilities are suggested. Like on a large strip of land, you can set up a tennis court or a volleyball pitch. And in the aft area called 'giardinetto' (which in Italian means both 'ship's quarter' and 'small garden') you can grow all kinds of vegetables. WallyIsland carries two Wally 47 tenders. You end up with a yacht 100 metres in length with the equivalent volume of a 60-metre guaranteeing unthinkable performance with the advantage that cost corresponds to volume, not overall length. The longer length on the waterline and the sharp bow make the boat faster. It is less affected by waves and can stay away from port longer. Not to mention the pleasure and comfort of living spaces set out on one level only. The enormous bilge

remains topical, contemporary. Wally development is therefore potential, there are no limits to the field. The first expression was yachts and the second, though far less extensive, was skis. We are often asked, especially by young people, to do other things: a motorbike, a jacket, a pair of sunglasses... so they can have symbols of that mixture of glamour, comfort and technology which distinguishes as excellent the definition of all the functions represented. One example was our decision

means that great quantities of fuel can be taken on, and the vast saloons lend themselves well to the most disparate uses: for example as an itinerant exhibition of prestigious art collections. In the basic version, in steel, it will have a highly industrial look, with the windows slightly inclined inwards like those of an airport control tower. But remember, Wally isn't a shipyard, a boat industry or anything else. The brand expresses a way of doing things, and in this sense doing means conceiving, where the design is functional, form for function. It comes about naturally in order to solve problems and improve functions, so it is not bound to time but always

"I don't' believe I'm artist. I'm more a rational but passionate conceiver of products."

to simplify the sail plan rather than resolve automation of the running rigging by means of hydraulic systems. This meant that you could tack by exploiting the wind alone, putting both sails on the other tack which were then suitably trimmed using the above systems. Others have merely automated, with considerable operational complications involved. Whereas our design optimises the combination of

because in reality the sections show an almost flat bottomed hull, whereas the vertical bow maintains V-sections, and the longer the waterline the faster and more sea-kindly the boat, the less she thumps the water. And if the deck is soaked by spray it doesn't really matter because at high speeds you're always sheltered. Our boats optimise the engine function, make a passage in the shortest possible time and offer the best of onboard comfort. We had already opted for

functions. Problems should be tackled at the root. That's why the vertical bow of our powerboats is not merely a distinguishing feature. Nor is it a search for the new just because it's new. It has a precise reason behind it. The main function of a powerboat is undoubtedly to travel fast. The limitations are two: power and sea conditions. The first can be resolved: bigger budget, more horsepower. The second must be tackled with a hull that best reacts to waves and allows you to maintain speed even with a sea running. In traditional boats the rake of the bow, the sharp profile, gives the sensation of cutting through the sea. A false sensation,

the vertical bow—which lengthens the waterline—on sailboats where speed is directly proportional to waterline length. Wally design is seen to be even more form for function in its micro expressions. We were the first to install retractable equipment that left the deck free, improving its appearance. But the main reason was to eliminate the possibility, especially in the case of guests, of inadvertently tripping up. Further obstructions are eliminated by running sheets and halyards below deck. Stowed forward, so far from the centre of balance, the anchor was a weight on the bow and moreover interrupted the clean line of the hull. We set the anchor inside the yacht, in a watertight box closer to the centre of balance, and it is dropped from below, also lessening the amount of chain paid out. A tube prevents the chain from touching the hull. The lifelines are formed by a combination of stanchions and cable stays and here, where a stay reached a pulpit—there are generally three—you needed a tensioning device for the cables, a terminal, a joint and a split-pin. Encumbering and dangerous things which in fact were covered with a stitched leather sheath to protect people's hands and also the sails. We invented a very easily adjustable system set inside the pulpits so that the stay emerged clean, without any tensioning mechanism. Details which at first sight may not be noticed. Then when one has recourse to typically architectural terms one speaks of 'functionalism,' but it should be kept in mind that for us the function is not an absolute but always the outcome of multiple, excellent performances whose meaning is related to well-being, to living in the best ways. An exquisitely epicurean meaning. So we don't identify with the attribute 'minimalist' because our way has nothing to do with labels: the design grows naturally, aimed at results of harmonious balance. On large vessels, for example, we do not use conventional guardrails and lifelines. Instead of ending at deck level, the hull continues up creating a solid raised bulwark. On vessels of less than 40 metres however the increased freebord created by the structure would be awkward rather than graceful. So Wally is a design of balance and coherency of functions. Our ideas give rise to products that reinvent the market while bearing the risk of not being immediately appreciated. They are indubitably long term. On the other hand ideas, system and strategy make the Wally brand stand out as exclusive. And this is reinforced by pursuing a course of constant experimentation. And this course identifies Wally style and behaviour, the representation of a private luxury, highly attentive to all performance values."

Decio Giulio Riccardo Carugati

"My father taught me as a child to understand you can make something beautiful or ugly for the same cost."

BIBLIOGRAPHY Enzensberger, Hans Magnus, *Zig Zag, The Politics of Culture and Vice Versa*, The New Press, New York 1999.

Classics of Today

The development of the Wally line of sailing yachts is part of the long and great tradition of innovation in yacht design dating back over the many centuries that man has been sailing the oceans.

There has been a continuous relationship between man's navigation and the sea as a source of food through fishing, of trade with the transport of people and goods, as a theatre of war and as a place of leisure and recreation.

All these different aspects of navigation have demonstrated man's resourcefulness and invention together with a ready desire to exploit new materials and technology.

The design imperative is very often driven by the search for speed. To be the first to fishing grounds and the first back with the catch like the bluenose schooners of Nova Scotia, or delivering the tea from the Far East in the tea race from Shanghai to London in the great clipper ships like the Cutty Sark in 1869. This search for speed has also been the major influence in the design of yachts for recreation, and particularly racing, which has a long and rich tradition as the sport of Kings.

One of the first recorded yachts built purely for pleasure was the 16 m (52 ft) sloop, Mary, given to Charles II of England in 1661 as a present from the Dutch East India Company. Mary was a replica of a Dutch man of war with eight guns and a crew of thirty. Charles raced his brother James Duke of York in 1661 in one of the first recorded races. It was from Greenwich to Gravesend and back, on the Thames. The Duke won the outer leg, the King the return, for a wager of £100.

Within a few months the King ordered a new yacht be built in an English shipyard with a design more suited to the less sheltered British waters and during his lifetime Charles II went on to build and own no less than twenty-eight similar vessels.

Charles II had a scientific outlook, founding the Royal Society in 1660, and so was always looking for improvements in his yachts. And of course it was no simple coincidence that fast safe boats were also important for the politics of trade and war. Mastery of yacht design and the sea has been the foundation of many great trading empires throughout history from the Phoenicians to the Greeks, the Romans, the Spanish, the Portuguese, the Dutch and the British.

When the first Wallygator was launched in 1991, the Wally team were following in this rich yachting tradition.

To understand why the phenomenon of Wally has had such a great influence on the market in such a short time one needs to examine how leisure yachting and particularly the sport of yacht racing has evolved.

The acknowledged Golden Age of Yachting was at the turn of the 20th century when yacht racing was very much the sport of Kings. It is no doubt that the elegance of the yachts designed at this time by naval architects like G. L Watson, Charles E. Nicholson, Nathaniel Herreshoff and William Fife is the reason why they still survive today.

In 1893 G. L. Watson designed Britannia for Queen Victoria's son Edward, Prince of Wales. Britannia was one of the most successful racing yachts of her era with 231 wins in 635 races between 1893 and 1935.

In 1881 Watson read a paper at the Exhibition of Naval Architecture and Marine Engineering at Glasgow. "We have not exhausted the possibilities of form yet, and when we do arrive at perfection of shape we can set-to then and look out for better material," said Watson."The frames and beams, then, of my ideal ship shall be of aluminium, the plating below the waterline of manganese bronze and the topsides of aluminium while I think it would be well to deck her, too, with that lightest of metals as good yellow pine will soon be only seen in museums."

Watson's relentless search for lightness, strength and speed with the introduction of new materials and building techniques, was readily evident. Just the same challenge is presented to the Wally designers today.

The shipyards on the Clyde were not yet ready to work with these new materials and the

37 m (121 ft) Britannia was fortunately (for her resultant longevity) built of American elm and pitch pine on steel frames.

It was the American designer Nathaniel Herreshoff, "the Wizard of Bristol," who adopted Watson's construction ideas with the building of Defender in 1895 for an America's Cup syndicate. Unfortunately the hull with bronze plating below water, and topsides and deck in aluminium started to dissolve with electrolysis as soon as it was launched into salt-water, probably the most expensive battery ever built.

Like the introduction of the Wally hull profiles, it was some time before Britannia's lines became accepted. At her launching in 1893 Dixon Kemp, the leading yachting commentator of the time, called Britannia's bow "gratuitously ugly" saying: "The form of the stem is a matter of taste ... but the uneducated eye of the rising generation, untrammelled by comparisons, will grow to love the Viking stem just as past generations did the Swan stem."

In addition to advances in materials and building technology, developments in yacht design have been very much influenced by changes in the rating rules of yacht racing where considerable financial investment is spent in trying to gain an advantage.

Throughout the history of yacht racing, rating rules have been introduced from time to time, primarily as a way of ensuring more equitable racing between craft of different designs.

This, however, often leads to type forming of designs in a particular direction as the designers endeavour to exploit the rule to seek every small advantage for their clients. The Yacht Racing Association Rule of 1880, for instance, led to rather impractical deep keeled, very narrow yachts with a beam to length ratio of 8 to 1, compared with modern yachts with a typical ration of 4 to 1, as the designers drew extreme yachts to exploit a particular loophole in the rule.

Previously the reserve of royalty and the very wealthy, yachting and yacht racing became gradually more readily accessible during the 20th century as wealth filtered down through society and more leisure time became accessible. This led to a long period of design development with smaller and less expensive yachts.

Once again it was competitive yacht racing, and in particular the new sport of ocean racing, that drove the designers to experiment with ideas in sail plans, hull shapes and new materials.

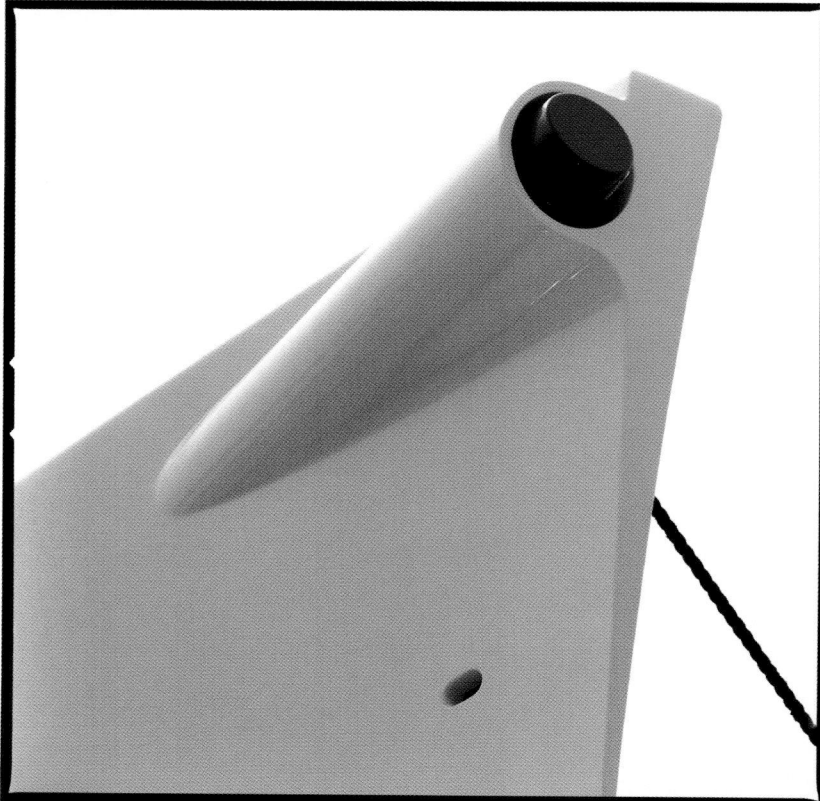

The most successful design team of this period was that of the American brothers Olin and Rod Stephens and their partner, Drake Sparkman. The Sparkman & Stephens 15 m (53 ft) yawl Dorade, built in 1930, won both the 1931 Transatlantic and Fastnet races and was followed by Stormy Weather as a Fastnet winner in 1935. For these designs S&S combined narrower beam, lighter construction and a Bermudian yawl rig rather than the gaff mainsails and schooner rigs seen on most yachts of the day.

On the European side, British designer Jack Laurent Giles designed a succession of yachts for John Illingworth, the top ocean racing skipper of the day. The 12 m (37 ft) Myth of Malham, winner of the 1947 Fastnet and hailed as a rule cheater, was the most influential design of the immediate post war years with more beam than the norm, higher freeboard, deep draft and shortened ends.

The masthead Bermudian cutter rig of Myth of Malham, in particular, exploited the new RORC Rating Rule where area of the foretriangle, in front of the mast, was excessively

cheap in rating terms compared with the size of the sail set there, and the mainsail. This led to a prolonged period where larger foresails were encouraged by the rating rules.

The long period of political stability and sustained economic growth after the Second World War encouraged all forms of recreational yachting including dinghy sailing, coastal and offshore cruising and ocean racing. New manmade materials helped to fuel this interest with Terylene and Dacron sails replacing canvas and cotton, giving more stable shape and far less weight aloft. New materials were also introduced into hull construction with Carl Beetle exhibiting the first fibreglass boat, a small sailing catboat dinghy, at the 1947 New York Boat Show and legendary British designer and sailor Uffa Fox developing the Flying Twenty, moulded in a combination of Crystic 189 polyester resin with matted glass fibres in 1952. Yacht design also moved ahead, stimulated as always by competition, as the new

biennial international offshore team racing series, the Admiral's Cup, first sailed in Cowes in 1957, brought together owners and designers from all over the world

One of these was American Dick Carter, a Yale graduate who designed the 1965 Fastnet Race winner, the 10 m (32 ft) Rabbit, as a "split keeler"; that is with the fin keel separated from a spade rudder hung well aft. Although this was not a new idea it very quickly led to the end of the long deep keels with the rudder hung on the trailing edge. Carter returned to the Admiral's Cup in 1969 with the even more radical 12.8 m (42 ft) Red Rooster, described by Carter as "the ultimate RORC Rule boat" with a pivoting keel varying the draft from 0.9 m to 2.7 m (2 ft 9 in to 9 ft). Red Rooster was top individual scorer and romped home to win the Fastnet.

These successes led to the establishment of the new International Offshore Rule, the IOR, in 1970 bringing together the British RORC Rule and the CCA rule of the USA. Carter, originally an advocate, ended up one of the greatest critics of the new IOR rule which penalised lifting keelers and centreboarders with massive penalties thereby effectively ending further development.

Rating Rules have always had to tread a fine balance between protecting the investment in the existing fleet and stifling innovation and experimentation, in the attempt to create fair and equal racing between yachts of diverse design and size.

The success of Admiral's Cup racing let to exposure for a whole new crop of designers like German Frers, Ron Holland, Doug Peterson, Ed Dubois, Jean-Marie Finot, Bruce Farr and Philippe Briand.

However, the limitations on the size of yachts allowed to compete in the Admiral's Cup led to some of the successful owners looking more intensively for line honours in the great ocean races like the Bermuda Race, the Sydney Hobart, the Fastnet and the Middle Sea Race to build bigger boats. In the late 1970s and 1980s these owners started building maxi racing yachts at the maximum size of around 24 m (80 ft) that the IOR rule allowed, with a resulting series of famous ocean racers like Boomerang, Kialoa, Il Moro di Venezia and Matador.

The IOR was ousted by the new IMS rule in 1989 that allowed boats even larger than 24 m (80 ft) to compete in ocean races, but still the design restrictions within the rule ended up producing slow, unstable and ugly boats that required upwards of thirty-five crew to sail them around the courses.

Outside of the limitations of these rating rules, designers have found plenty of opportunity to design fast yachts, again stimulated by competition such as the single-handed races around the world and across the Atlantic.

Racing multihulls and monohulls designed for these races without major restrictions, has led to major advances in construction, sail plans, equipment and underwater appendages.

These yachts have set some phenomenal new sailing records such as the outright 24 hour distance record in 2006 by Bruno Peyron in the 36 m (120 ft) catamaran Orange II of 766.8 nautical miles at an average speed of 31.95 knots or the west to east Transatlantic monohull record of 6 days and 17 hours set by the 42.6 m

(140 ft) ketch Mari Cha IV in 2003 at an average speed of 18.05 knots.

The demands of cruising yacht design, again without any rating rule restrictions, has led to reductions in draft with lifting keels and bulb keels and innovation in sail handling equipment to reduce crew numbers with captive hydraulic winches to handle the high sheet loads on the sailing superyachts and sail furling systems.

It is in the context of this long tradition of innovation throughout yachting history that the Wally designs can be viewed.

The Wally story starts with the desire of accomplished racing yachtsman and businessman, Luca Bassani, to create the perfect boat for his own exacting requirements of a performance cruising yacht that could be sailed with the minimum of crew.

Unable to find anything suitable on the market, he set up a process of analysing each

element of his requirements, finding solutions that avoided compromises in performance, comfort or style and then started building the result of his research.

The outcome has been a succession of remarkable boats including the ketch Wallygator, Genie of the Lamp, Tiketitan, the WallyTender and the awesome 60-knot gas turbine powered 118 WallyPower.

The Wally timing, at the start of the 1990s, was just right. Firstly, new materials for hull construction, spars and sails were just becoming available and new ideas on keels and ballast arrangements were being tested on the racing circuits.

Secondly, yachtsmen around the world were beginning to look for something different from the overcrowded decks of the racing maxis and the over complicated, slow and uninspiring cruising yachts on offer.

Starting with a blank sheet where everything was possible Wally looked at every aspect of the performance and the use of a yacht, sometimes developing successful ideas from the past and sometimes coming up with completely new solutions as they addressed the major design challenges of performance, safety and ease of use.

The result has been a radical new design concept of yachts that has changed the way that they are enjoyed and has had an effect on all the other manufacturers and designers, and all the yachts built since.

Starting with the technical aspects of performance and functionality in hull design, sail plan and equipment, the Wally team then looked at all the social requirements of a yacht from ease of boarding and where to sunbathe, to the interior layout, and then, finally, they integrated all these ideas into a totally elegant and stylish finished product.

One of the most exciting and far-reaching aspects of the new Wally design phenomenon that has had a far-reaching consequence in the history of yacht design, has been the new approach taken to social life on board a yacht.

In the years since building the first boat, Wally has redesigned almost every part and every system used on a boat so that Wally's are now totally unique in every aspect.

Beyond the stunning looks there is a high level of integrity and a respect of the heritage of yachting in the designs that make them the classics of today. With Wally, the yachting future is now.

Jason Holtom

wally is

THE FIRST TIME YOU SEE A WALLY
YOU IMMEDIATELY KNOW
THAT YOU ARE LOOKING
AT AN OBJECT OF PURE DESIRE.
ASPIRATIONAL, INSPIRATIONAL
AND INNOVATIVE, THE WALLY FLEET
ARE THE UNDISPUTED MASTERS
OF YACHTING'S HAUTE COUTURE.

*The consistent theme across the brand, reflecting
the continuity of sailing and the sea, is that simplicity
is a virtue and that you should make technology work for you.*

Throughout the Wally design process
the aesthetics are an integral part of the result, not the reason
for the process, where form definitely follows function.
Technical equipment such as cleats and bollards are concealed
and there is no superfluous embellishment or detailing
to distract from the environment.
Wally is not designing just to be different, there has to be
a purpose, to create something better.

WALLY DESIGNS HAVE COMPLETELY CHANGED THE EXPECTATIONS
OF LEISURE YACHTING AND THE WAY THAT YACHTS
ARE ENGINEERED AND CONSTRUCTED.
WALLY HAS REDEFINED THE GENRE OF LARGE CRUISING YACHTS
AND HOW TO ENJOY THE SEA, AND HAS TAKEN THE LIFESTYLE
AND GRACE OF EARLIER YACHTING ERAS AND BROUGHT THEM RIGHT
UP TO DATE. THEN SHOWN THE WAY INTO THE FUTURE.

THE WALLY APPROACH IS

TO ALWAYS CHALLENGE

THE ACCEPTED BOUNDARIES,

SEEKING NEW SOLUTIONS

TO THE AGE-OLD PROBLEMS

OF NAVIGATING THE SEAS,

FROM MINIMISING

THE UNDERWATER DRAG

OF THE APPENDAGES TO NEAT

STOWAGE OF THE TENDER;

ALL FOR THE ULTIMATE

COMFORT OF THE OWNER

AND GUESTS.

"Wally is a harmony of aesthetics, design and technological content that radically changed sailing and yachting twelve years ago, showing a new path that no one had ever dared to walk down."

Marco Tronchetti Provera, Kauris III

Great effort is spent finding the right solution for the best enjoyment; how to anchor quickly and easily, how to swim off the transom, how to board by tender, how to be safe and secure under sail, how to picnic in privacy and comfort, how to shelter from the sun and wind.

COLOUR-CODED IN SPECIALLY FORMULATED METALLIC PAINT FINISHES FROM THE TOP OF THEIR TOWERING CARBON MASTS TO THE MATCHING SUPPORT TENDERS, WALLY YACHTS STAND OUT FOR THE END OF MEDIOCRITY.
WALLY DESIGNS LOOK DIFFERENT, THEY ALSO LOOK RIGHT; CONTEMPORARY, EXCLUSIVE, DESIRABLE, FAST AND FIT FOR THE PURPOSE. SLEEK MODERNITY, YET WITH A SENSE OF CRAFT AND TIMBER.

UNMISTAKABLE SILKY-SMOOTH STYLING MAKES
A WALLY SAILING YACHT LOOK FAST EVEN WHEN
IT IS MOORED AT THE DOCKSIDE.
OUT ON THE WATER THE CLARITY OF THE VISION
IS EMPHASISED WITH THE EASY GRACE AND PACE
THAT THE WALLY SAILING YACHTS ACHIEVE
UNDER SAIL WITH
THE MINIMUM OF FUSS.

*The Wally fleet are the only modern yachts allowed along
the quayside of the Old Port during the fashionable
Les Voiles de Saint Tropez classic regatta.
The Wally classics for the 22nd century lie easily alongside
the gleaming varnish, brass and forest of rigging
of the magnificently restored classics of the masters of yacht
design of the first half of the 20th century
like William Fife, G. L. Watson,
Charles Nicholson and Nathaniel Herreshoff.*

My Magic Carpet[2] is a source
of pride and joy.
Watching her sail up the Gulf
of Saint Tropez (for once without
me on board) her speed and beauty
can still take my breath away.
Everyone says 'she is truly magical'
but only I know why.
From the same spot, I used
to watch the classic maxi racers
and then think: ten crew just
for an afternoon sail—no way.
It is not a question of money,
it is a question of freedom.
Then one day I went on board
my first Wally and in thirty seconds
I knew this was the way forward.
A unique combination
of technology and design
but above all, here is a boat we can
sail faster than those maxis but
with a crew—for a day sail —of only
two. And look—no ropes to trip over!
This is the magic of Wally,
for which I shall always
be grateful to Luca Bassani:
Wally reconciled my family
with sailing."

Sir Lindsay Owen-Jones, Magic Carpet[2]

simplicity

Wallys sail with minimal crew compared with their maxi counterparts. Hoisting sails, tacking, reefing and anchoring can be carried out by just one person with touch button control from the security of the helm station.

Looking across the teak-laid decks you wonder where have all the winches gone, where are all the ropes, where are those hard steel tracks, fittings and rails lying in wait to stub the unwary toe.

"Wally changed the way of sailing, transforming it into an experience of technology, aesthetics, research and lightness. Without Wally it would have been very difficult for us to have become so passionate about the sailing world."

Owner Shaka

the art of the deck, it's all in the detail

Flush decks invented by Wally for cruising yachts maintain the purity of the lines and make it easy and safe to walk around creating additional areas for sunbathing and relaxing.

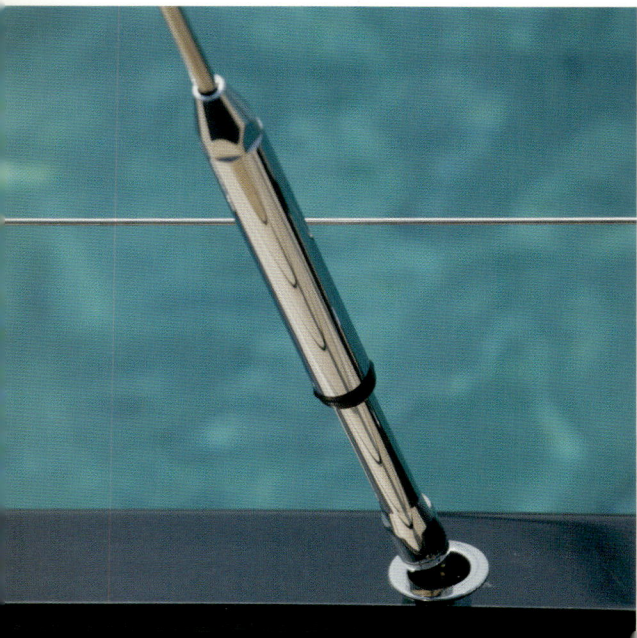

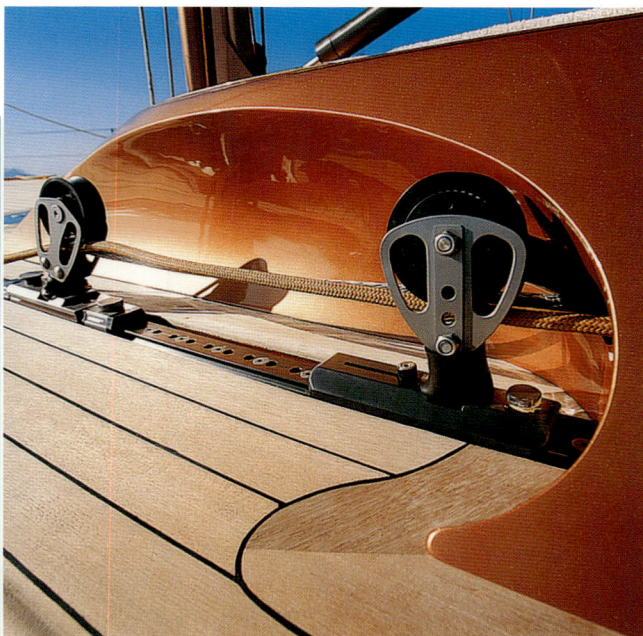

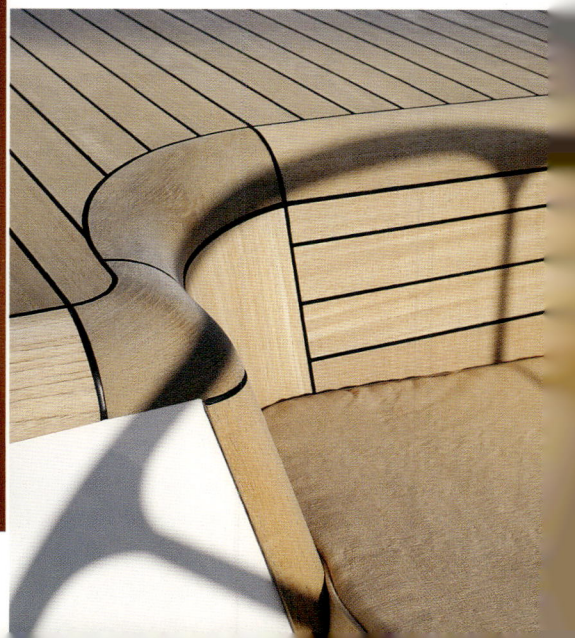

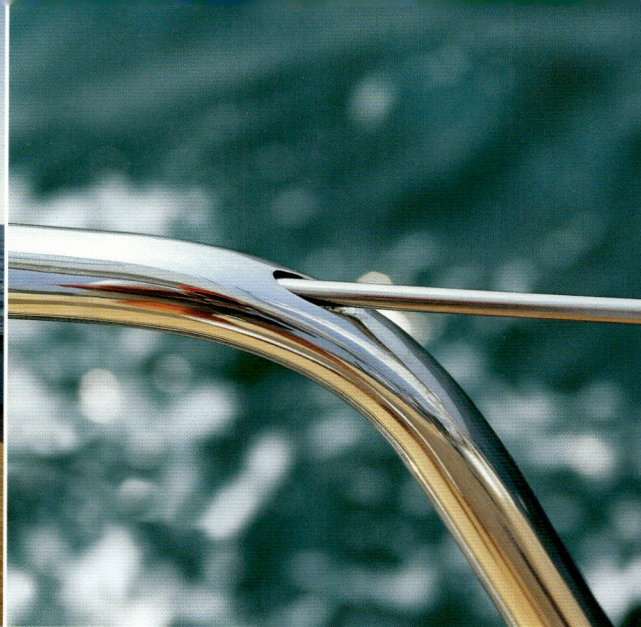

Simplicity and functionality have been applied to the layout of the deck so that there is nothing to distract the eye from the sea views.

Every item of deck hardware from mooring cleat to stanchion is integrated into the design and when possible concealed to leave the teak-laid decks safe and unobstructed.

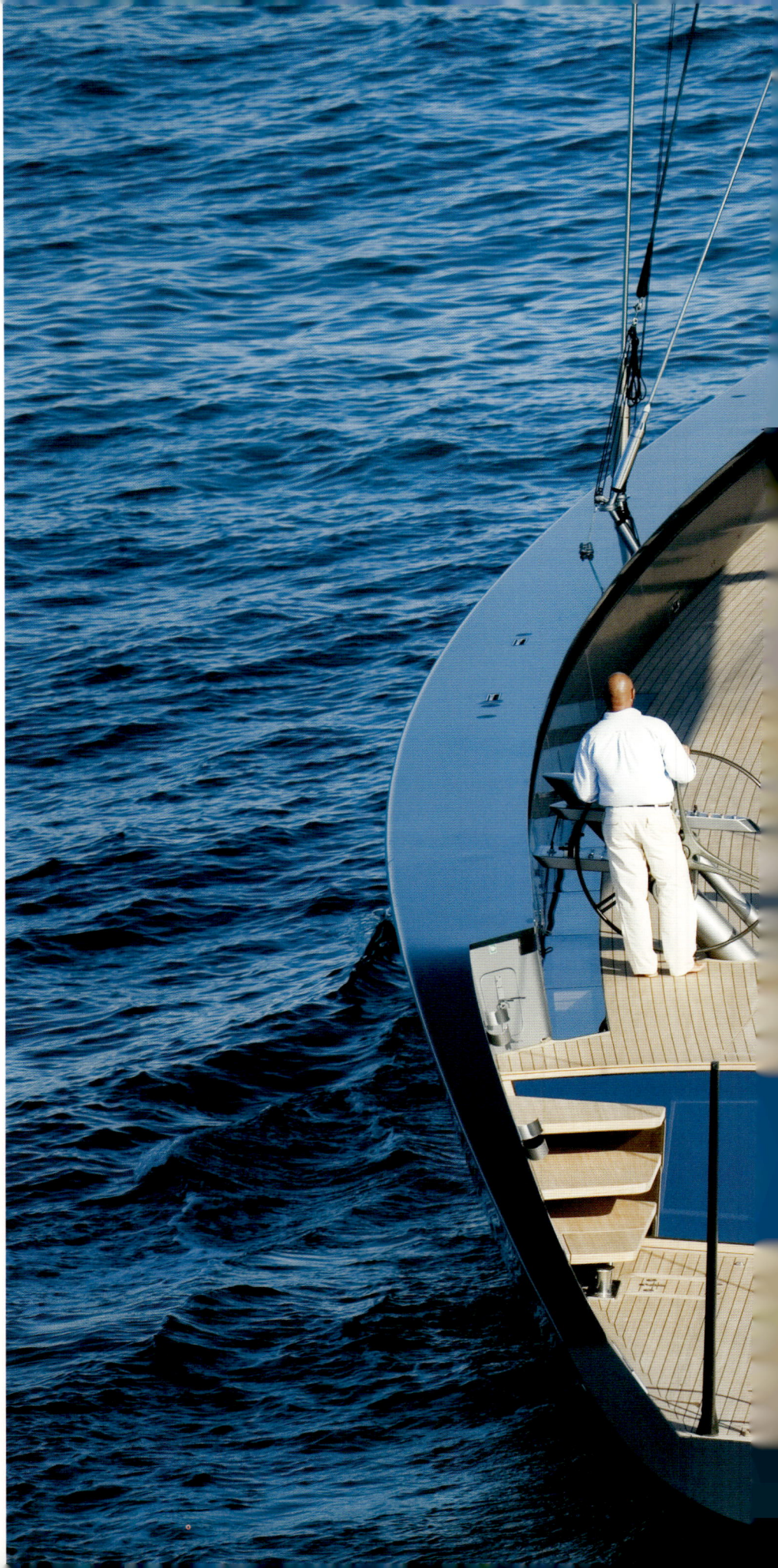

"I remember the first time. The meeting with a sculptured shape of unusual lines, harmonic, capable of profoundly changing the guidelines with which I had, up until that moment, envisaged my life at sea.

It happened by chance.

An unplanned visit.

The curiosity aroused by a beauty met in Summertime and remaining in the mind's eye.

So we had words.

I knew the story of the man who had dedicated his own life to a passion and I understood then how he had succeeded in entering this subject, and then modelled it for the wind.

Very little time passed.

We found ourselves sitting around a table in order to give shape to a project that I would discover to be magnificent. This person, who showed himself to be above all more than human, was the founder of creativity and thoughts that filled the days with a growing common interest, enriching the people around him and working together towards a creation for the sea that tends towards the future but in its soul remains the love for tradition."

Owner Esense

"LESS IS MORE" IS A CONSISTENT THEME IN THE
DEVELOPMENT AT WALLY. AS IN THE MINIMAL
REQUIREMENT FOR SAILING CREW, THE AIM IS
ENJOY THE SEA WITHOUT DISTRACTIONS.
SIMPLICITY IS THE RAISON D'ETRE.
NOTHING IS SUPERFLUOUS, OSTENTATIOUS
OR DECORATIVE.

the bottom line

Wally's underwater

anchor system

keeps the bow neat

and uncluttered.

It removes the weight

and complication

of a bow roller

as well as reducing

the amount

of chain required and

moves the weight

aft to decrease pitching.

Yam is our first sailing yacht, we previously had owned various motor boats. Our children love sailing, also at a competitive level, we therefore decided to change and opt for a sailing yacht. What a shame we had not done so before!

For me it is very important that I can identify myself with the objects that I own, whether it be a car, a watch or a piece of clothing. They must all 'tell me something' every time I look at them or use them.

With Wally it was like this from the very first moment, from when Luca Bassani presented me with the 'Wally Idea' at the beginning of our discussions.

Wally unites in a rational and balanced design, performance, functionality and obviously safety, which are the three main parameters for a yacht. It manages to be classic and innovative at the same time.

Wally has created something new. If a boat built ten or fifteen years ago seems very old in her design, this is due above all to Wally, a concept that many other shipyards for both small and large yachts have copied."

Michael Levi, Yam

performance

"Speed. More than Hurry," advertising campaign 1996

Design objectives include a fast, easily driven hull shape for enjoyable and safe passage making in both light and heavy airs, a deck layout for easy sail handling with minimum crew and maximum space for open air relaxation at sea and at anchor.

The importance of performance led Wally to develop light displacement and advanced composite construction creating a new generation of yachts that offer exceptional characteristics of comfort, safety and performance in style.

"World's fastest superyacht project.

I believe that the Wally 130, scheduled to be completed in January 2008, merged the concepts developed by Wally and myself in perfect harmony.

Performance, comfort, simplicity and at the same time aggressive design, have all been integrated through 'state of the art' technology.

The new Wally 130 is going to be my third sailing yacht from Wally.

My first Wally, the Wally 100 Dark Shadow was great for cruising.

My second, the Wally 60 Wallyño is fast and sporty.

Unlike any other Wally sailing yacht ever built, the Wally 130 is considered to be the most innovative of Wally's fleet.

Wally is designing and building a new generation of extraordinary, refined, hi-performance cruising sailing yachts that have never been seen before.

I would like to praise Wally for its achievement in opening new doors to the world of sailing yachts."

Kazuo Akao, Wallyño and Wally 130

lightness of the soul

Weight is the enemy of speed. Wally has developed the most advanced composite construction technology with high strength and lightweight laminates.

Wally is the world leader in advanced composites, building yachts with carbon fibre that are lighter making then faster and easier to sail with reduced loads.

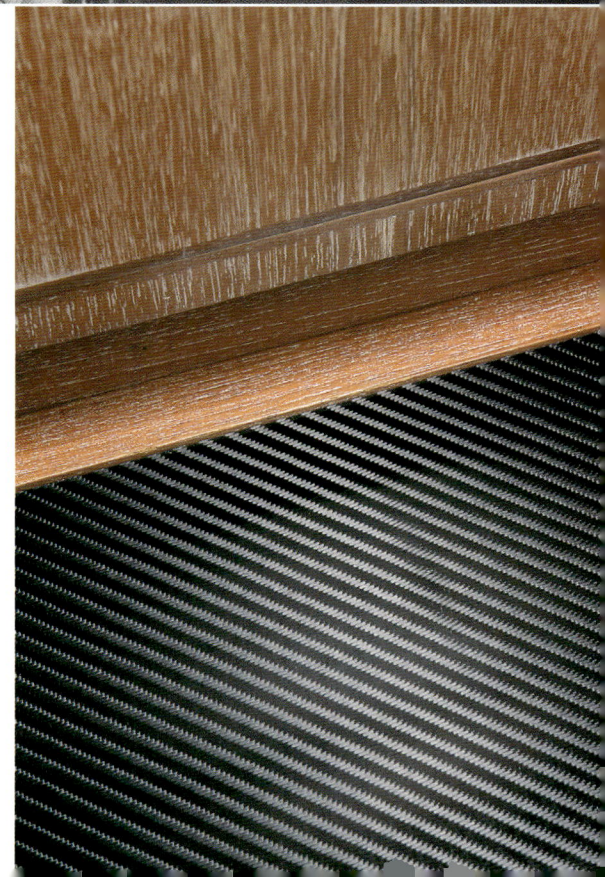

fast and easy

"At Ease. More than in Love," advertising campaign 1998

AT A TIME WHEN MORE AND MORE
CRUISING YACHTS RELY ON THE MOTOR
IN LIGHT AIRS, WALLY OWNERS CELEBRATE
THE JOY OF SAILING WITH YACHTS
THAT ARE BOTH FAST AND EASY TO SAIL.

**THE EASILY DRIVEN HULL SHAPE
DEVELOPED IN THE TEST TANK
IS COMPLEMENTED BY THE LIGHT
DISPLACEMENT OF ADVANCED
COMPOSITE CONSTRUCTION
THAT SAVES UP TO 45 PER CENT
OF THE WEIGHT OF A YACHT BUILT
IN CONVENTIONAL MATERIALS.**

HIGH-LIFT LOW-DRAG UNDERWATER
APPENDAGES AND EFFICIENT
HIGH ASPECT SAIL PLANS MAKE
THE BOATS PRECISE AND RESPONSIVE
AND A DELIGHT ON THE HELM.

the sail plan

High aspect sail plans
designed for performance
and ease of handling
with minimal crew.

Wally introduced
the self-tacking jib to large
cruising yachts for fast and easy
automatic tacking with
push-button control trimming
so that one person can sail
the yacht.

Wally was the first to use carbon
sailcloth for cruising yachts
developing 3DL technology to give
the ultimate in lightweight,
durability, performance and style.
Sails that are easier to handle
and hold their shape for longer.

Colourful asymmetric
gennakers for fast downwind
sailing that are simple to set
and gybe with no pole required
and just one set of sheets
for trimming.

Performance is exceptional with the Wallys able to sail faster than the wind speed in light airs. In heavier airs off wind speeds in excess of 20 knots are possible with full control.
The ease and speed that allows you to instantly raise the anchor and set sail at the touch of a button has transformed sailing from a chore into an absolute pleasure.
The combination of onboard systems that make setting, trimming and stowing of sails so easy and the light displacement hulls that perform in the full range of wind conditions mean that Wally owners sail most of the time. Wally heaven: the real pleasure of getting there under sail.

WALLY IS: Dreams, vision, technology, creativity and knowledge made into reality.

Wally represents the ultimate design, created by advanced thinking, realised today. As for my Wally 105, S/Y Nariida, she gives me and my family the pleasure of cruising and me and my friends the greatest racing, on a fast, fun and competitive boat."

Morten Sig. Bergesen, Nariida

push and go

Wally has pioneered hydraulic double-acting sheeting rams for push-button, instant, effort free control of mainsail and jib from the helm station.

Stowed neatly under deck coamings, the hydraulic rams offer one-man operation and remove all the clutter of winches and ropes.

Safety is improved with no highly loaded sheets allowing easy movement around the deck.

SINCE THE FIRST WALLY, THE 25 M (83 FT) WALLYGATOR WAS

LAUNCHED IN 1991, THE WALLY DESIGN SYSTEM AND STRATEGY

HAS CONTINUED TO EVOLVE WITH OCCASIONAL "REVOLUTIONS" SO

THAT SUCCESSIVE MODELS CONSTANTLY CHALLENGE

THE ACCEPTED VIEW OF THE MARKET AND OFFER IMPROVED

AND MORE REFINED SOLUTIONS.

never ending

[re] evolution

Question, design, test, evolve; the Wally system is a continuous cycle, constantly striving to move forward with the resolve that you only carry on if you can do it better.

"

Here are a few emotions that we have experienced
in the Wally world. Participating in regattas
in the Wally Class we have greatly appreciated
the extraordinary technological talents of Wally
that unites innovative design; it has transformed
the world of Yachting.
Particularly exhilarating is the moment of acceleration
as the wind fills the sails giving a feeling of 'take off.'
The competitive experience has also been useful
and educational for the children who have started
to understand the value of teamwork, of concentration
and being professional. Whilst cruising, we have spent
some wonderful holidays with the entire family thanks
to the versatility of the yacht, that allows
the co-habiting of the central deck house,
and the youngsters with their friends use with great
enthusiasm the 'terrace on the sea.' The layout, that
includes the aft terrace, is full of light and sea views
and is a very effective and creative solution
and extremely pleasant in all seasons.
Agility and speed are the qualities that have allowed
us to move easily around the Mediterranean with
a small group of friends, keeping up even with...
the motor yachts. Long live Wally!"

Owner Tiketitan

testing times

Hydrodynamic tank testing of hulls and wind tunnel testing of rigs and superstructures
are used by Wally designers to reduce drag and improve performance.

The efficiency and sleek lines of the 118 WallyPower and the whole WallyPower range,
are the result of extensive R&D that included tank testing at the SSPA facility in Göteborg,
Sweden, and smoke testing in the Ferrari Wind Tunnel Facility in Maranello, Italy.

Wally sailing yachts are not just unique objects of design and style, they also combine a level of technology, performance and comfort that is unprecedented.

Wally brings the art of sailing into the 21st century and for me, is the ultimate way to enjoy the wind and the sea with my family."

Andrea Recordati, Indio

Alexia

researching and developing

"Solutions. More than loads", advertising campaign 1997

WALLY ADDRESSES THE DEVELOPMENT
OF EACH PRODUCT IN THE SAME WAY
WITH NO PRECONCEPTIONS. EVEN WHEN
THE RESULT IS ALWAYS MORE THAN
A "SIMPLE" PRODUCT, THE SOLUTION
IS SO OFTEN "SIMPLE" AND
UNCOMPLICATED. THE GUIDING PRINCIPLE
IS THAT IT IS ONLY WORTH DOING
SOMETHING IF IT IS AN IMPROVEMENT.

moveable ballast

Deep draft limits cruising
destinations; shallow draft limits
performance.

Wally has developed
a series of moveable ballast
systems for large yachts
to optimise performance
and cruising potential.

Canting keel, lifting keel
or water ballast;
the best solution is selected
for each project.

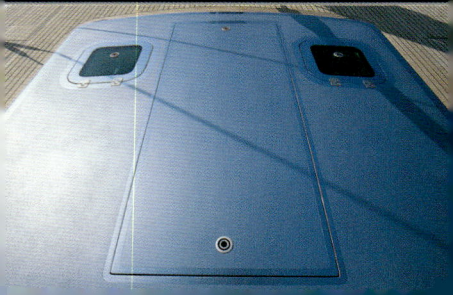

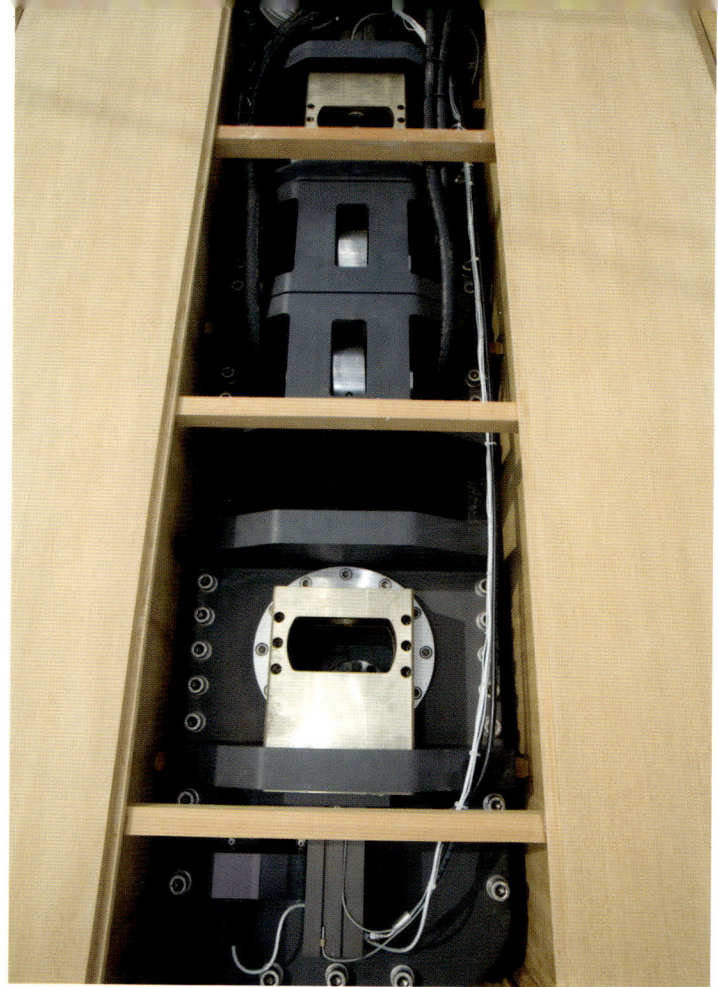

THE QUALITY IN THE WALLY BRAND GOES FAR DEEPER
THAN THE STYLING, THE SUPERB LEVEL OF FINISH,
THE ATTENTION TO DETAIL AND THE CRAFTSMANSHIP
EVIDENT IN THE PRODUCTS.

QUALITY STARTS WITH THE CREATIVE THINKING APPLIED
IN THE ORIGINAL RESEARCH AND DESIGN
AND IS THEN MAINTAINED THROUGHOUT THE ENGINEERING,
CONSTRUCTION AND FITTING-OUT PROCESS
TO CREATE THE MOST TECHNOLOGICALLY ADVANCED
YACHTS IN THE WORLD.

quality

"When I think about Wally I think about the only possible sailboat for a person with a feel for art and design. In my view you cannot separate Wally from Luca Bassani, he created the ideas, philosophy and the design 'language.'

At a later stage—when Wally had its own shipyard—the most surprising aspect for me was the ability of very many Wally employees to incorporate that vision into each new project. Wally has created something extraordinary, a new style which most probably will survive as a famous brand."

Thomas Bscher, Open Season

the rig

Swept back spreaders simplify the rigging for safer sailing, removing the need for crew and winches to control running backstays when tacking and gybing.

Composite PBO rigging is incredibly strong and light reducing both overall weight and weight aloft.

Durable lightweight advanced composite carbon spars lower the centre of gravity for more comfortable sailing with less pitching and increase the righting moment for better performance and reduced draft.

*WALLY OWNERS HAVE THE
SATISFACTION OF KNOWING THAT
EVERY SECTION OF THEIR BOAT HAS
BEEN SUBJECT TO A PROCESS OF
RELENTLESS THOUGHT AND
EVALUATION: WHEN A TECHNICALLY
SUPERIOR AND NEATER SOLUTION
IS FOUND, IT IS INCORPORATED.*

**The high level of innovation
applied in every stage of the
building process means that
much of the quality is hidden
beneath the surface in
the technical content and the
custom-designed engineering
systems and solutions.**

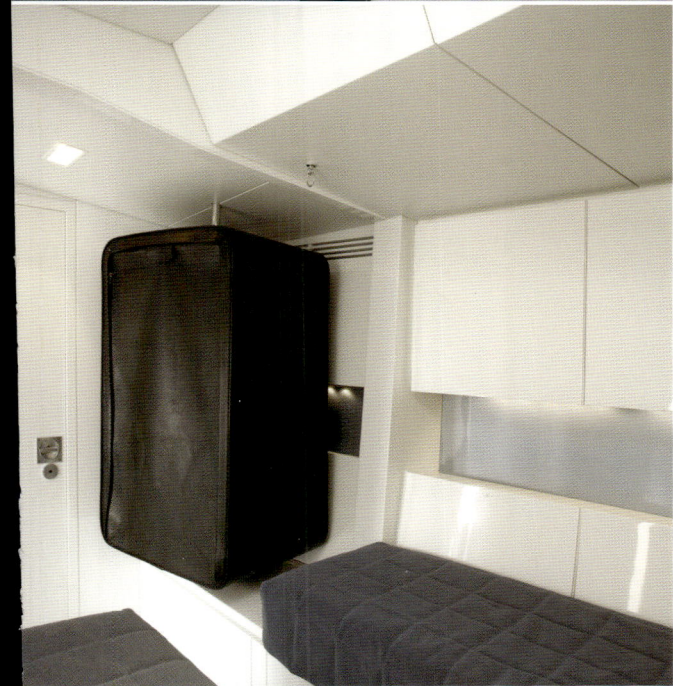

joined up thinking

The finely crafted interiors combine

lightweight cored wood laminates

and carbon composites created

in the custom joinery shops with

computer-aided design and cutting.

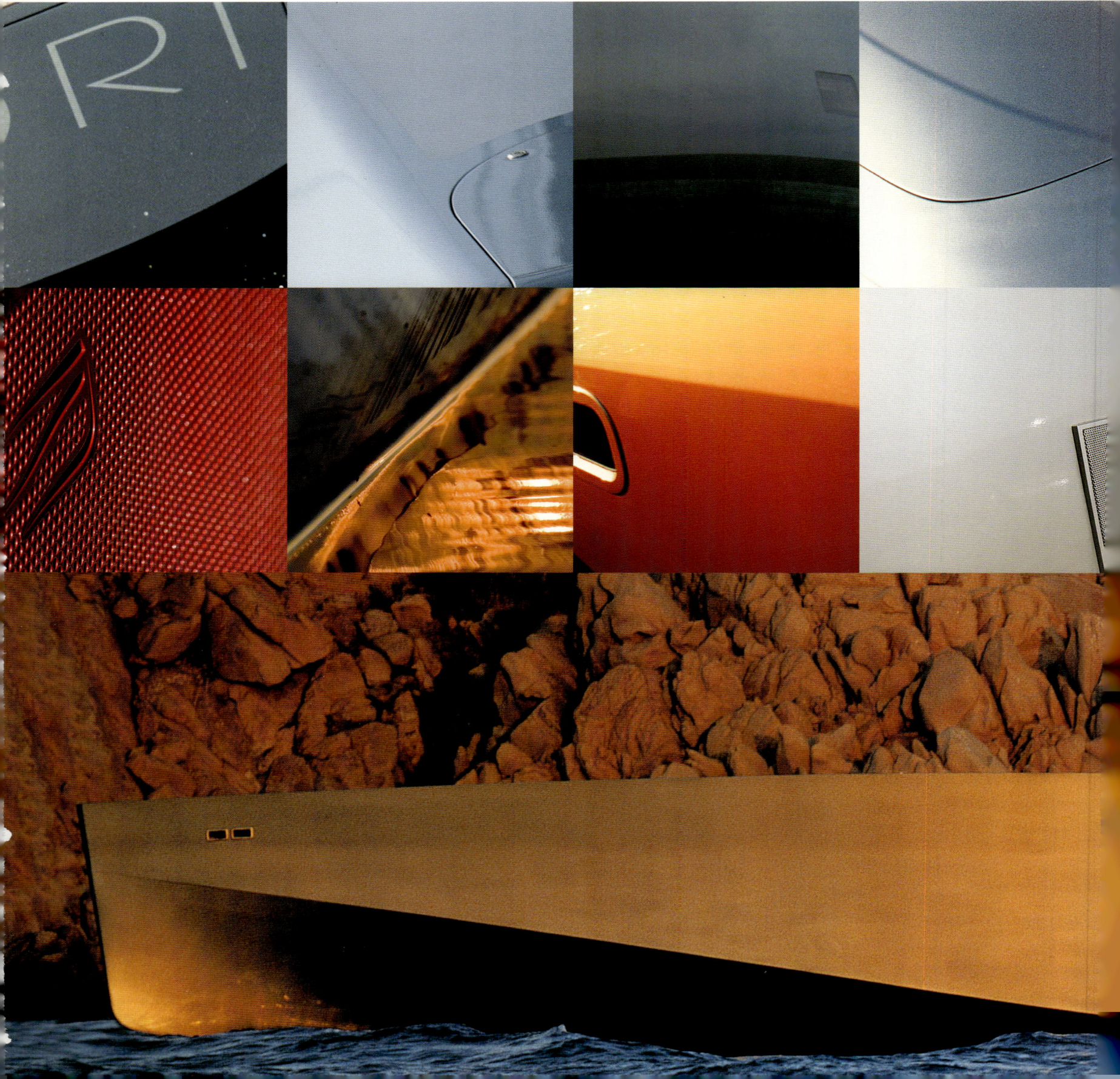

Wally single-colour

paint schemes

emphasise

the soul of each

project with special

metallic tones

creating a rainbow

of hues that reflect

the natural

everchanging

colours of the sea.

The Wally paint
technology offers
a choice of custom
pastel and
metallic colours for
individual expression

allowing the yachts to
blend naturally into
the marine
environment.

The aim is to keep

in harmony

with the environment

of the seascape and

the coastal landscape,

not conflict with it

or distract from it.

FROM CONCEPTION
TO COMPLETION, EVERY PART
OF THE WALLY EXPERIENCE
IS TO TASTE THE VERY ESSENCE
OF THE SEA. THIS INCLUDES
THE WAY THEY ARE BUILT,
THE WAY THEY LOOK,
THE WAY THAT
THEY ARE PROMOTED AND
THE WALLY CLASS REGATTAS
THAT BRING THE BOATS
AND THE OWNERS TOGETHER.

style

"Art. More than Beauty,"   *advertising campaign 1998*

My Wally: Beautiful and Different.

Why does every boat have to be white?

Why can my boat not be fast and easy?

Why can I not have a long lunch and still go for a short sail with my friends as the late afternoon sea breeze arrives?

Why do I have to stub my toe?

There is so much to like about my Wally.

The best is that you want it more after you have it.

More colour, more sail, more power, more speed, lighter, faster, quicker, beauty, most beautiful.

No one ever knew they wanted a Wally until Luca presented it to them. Now everyone wants one.

A Wally is a noun, but it will be an adjective."

Alex Jackson, Carrera

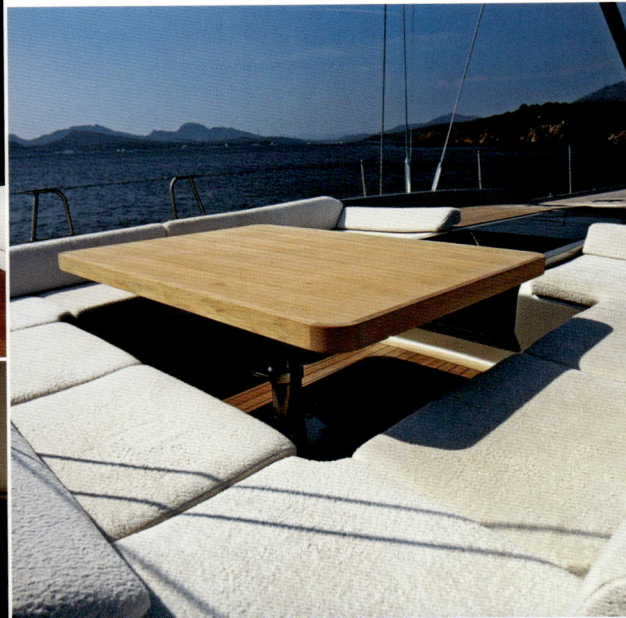

loft on the water

The versatility of the deck and interior social areas is a Wally lifestyle concept.

The freedom to modify the layout according to various situations and requirements has led to the development of designs that combine and integrate the different living spaces.

Salons with sliding tables maximise the useable area. Guest cabins with opening bulkheads increase the social space. Deck cockpits with lowering tables create wide sun pads. Outdoor modular components can be moved anywhere and anyway to live the whole deck.

Flexibility to change the moment.

the joys of wally

"Alone. But in Good Company," advertising campaign 1997

THE ULTIMATE SIMPLICITY OF "ONE-MAN, ONE-BOAT" GIVES A CLEAR VISION OF THE ENJOYMENT OF WALLY OWNERSHIP.

Designs that reflect the needs of the modern yachtsman, emphasising the importance of making the best of the time available for relaxation.

ALL WALLY YACHTS ARE DESIGNED TO BE PRACTICAL FOR THE OUTDOOR SAILING LIFESTYLE.

WALLY HAS PROVED THAT OWNERS NEED NOT FACE THE DILEMMA OF COMPROMISING COMFORT FOR PERFORMANCE.

"Wally revolutionised sailing. Sailing a Wally is not only sailing a challenging, fast and very comfortable boat, it is more: it is lifestyle, it is excitement. Wherever you sail on a Wally, the attention is on you whether you want it or not. The Wally team not only develop groundbreaking boats, they also establish a very special relationship with their owners. Whether it is racing, cruising or just hanging out, the Wally team is there and I always find them competent, careful and good fun. My best sailing experience... WALLY!"

Owner Tiketitoo

furling assets

Fully battened mainsails provide the best in performance with better control of shape and twist.

In-boom furling 3DL fully battened mainsail allows fast

and easy sail setting and reefing and neat stowage at the end of the day.

Wally has brought new sailing aspirations to
some of the most powerful and influential people
in the world, attracting a set of discerning
owners, some with years of yachting experience
others just dipping their toes into the water
for the first time attracted by the styling and the
whole new yachting experience.

WALLY OWNERS ENJOY BEING
PART OF THE INNOVATION
PROCESS, COMING BACK FOR A
SECOND AND THIRD TIME.

"Exhilarating to be at the helm of an object like my Tuamata, that with ease takes me speedily around my beloved Mediterranean, giving me moments of joy with her technology and the purity of her lines."

Claudio Luti, Tuamata

expanding views

Raised deep bulwarks
on the 118 WallyPower give
full protection when underway
and then at anchor
they can be hydraulically
lowered to broaden the view
from the saloon.

THE HEART OF THE WALLY EXPERIENCE
IS PROMOTING A LIFESTYLE
ON THE WATER BY COMBINING
PERFORMANCE WITH ALL
THE ESSENTIALS FOR COMPLETE
ENJOYMENT OF THE SEA.

lifestyle

"Comforts. More than Efforts," advertising campaign 1996

"Our adventure with Wally began ten years ago.

Already with a passion for sailing and the sea, having travelled around the world with other boats, my husband's and my own desire was to be able to repeat this experience with a boat that was technologically advanced and whose qualities matched up to our personal expectations.

The encounter with Wally allowed us to make our dream come true. We lived through the exhilarating experience of joining in the design process and witnessing the building of our Kenora.

Even if we were never able to travel around the world together, I continue to sail in other seas and Kenora continues to be the hotel of all my dreams."

Owner Kenora

pieds dans l'eau

The main saloon opens out aft into the unique "terrace-on-the-sea" set at sea level in the scooped out transom extending the interior space for inside outside living.

Creating a private cockpit, away from the technical areas of the boat, the "terrace" is the perfect sheltered retreat when sailing for relaxing, sunbathing and enjoying the view and all with direct access to the cool interior.

Introduced on Tiketitan, the lowered area makes access to the water easier for swimming and boarding from tenders when at anchor and opens up the sea views from the aft saloon.

Vision belongs to those who know how
to shape the future.
Because I believe that 'less is more' in life,
this statement perfectly reflects
for me Wally's
outstanding vision of the 21st century's
yachting industry.
Sailing a Wally is a combination
of pleasure, performance,
art and technology."

Jean-Charles Decaux, J One

communication

The Wally thinking is different
and refreshing.
The whole process of communication
reflects the Wally soul: new ways
of photographing boats, innovative
corporate identity, creative advertising
and essential graphic design.

Wally has stimulated the market with witty copy writing, in
addition to the strong photographic images of the boats.

COMMUNICATING THE WALLY MESSAGE FOLLOWS THE SAME
PIONEERING PATH AS THE DESIGN PROCESS: TAKING
ESTABLISHED IDEAS, ANALYSING THEM WITH CREATIVE THINKING
AND THEN COMBINING THEM WITH NEW CONCEPTS TO
PRODUCE SOMETHING THAT IS TOTALLY FRESH AND ORIGINAL.

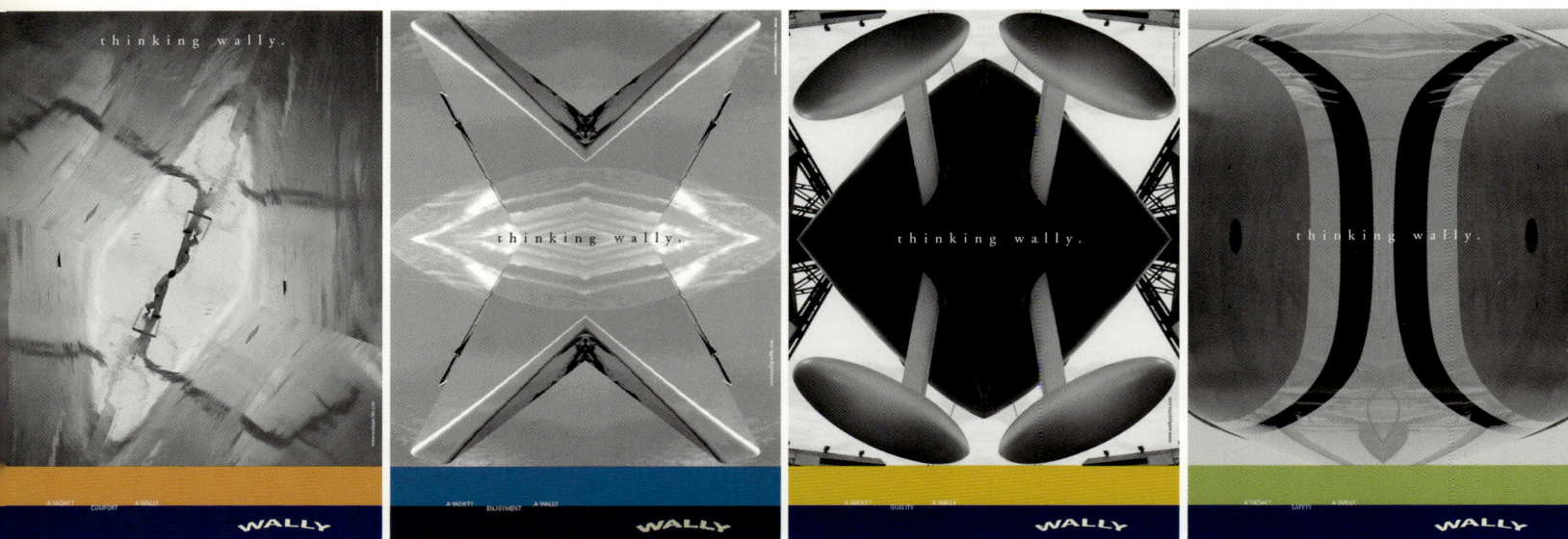

IN THE "THINKING WALLY" ADVERTISING CAMPAIGN
BLACK AND WHITE IMAGES OF PARTS
OF A BOAT UNDER CONSTRUCTION ARE PRESENTED
IN AN ABSTRACT WAY TO CREATE COMPLETELY
NEW CONCEPTS THAT ARE ARRESTING AND UNEXPECTED.

thinking wally
advertising campaign 1999

"

Wally yachts are an uncompromising blend of elegance, aesthetics, speed, comfort and ease of handling. Sailing them is a real thrill."

Domenico de Sole

Why did I dream about a Wally? It is a kind of 'Coup de Coeur.' You cannot explain it. I love sailing and sailing boats but I wanted a Wally. It is like a painting or any kind of art, you just feel that you were waiting for it. It was the link I wanted to enjoy the ultimate continent: the Big Blue.

I wanted my family to share with me the dream and the pleasure to be a Wally owner and organized a long weekend sail between Corsica and Italy. The first cruise on a new boat is always a magic moment. In the morning on a mirror-like sea, just as the sun was rising my skipper knocked on my cabin door to wake me up. I was wondering what happened when I heard him saying there was a big whale following the boat. I rushed out of bed and watched through the window of my cabin designed just above the water level... and the whale was there, swimming next to the boat, so close... It was like a warm welcome to Dark Shadow and my family. It was like the whale enjoyed watching my boat and the Wally magic touch. 'Bravo' to Wally who make dreams become reality!"

Owner Dark Shadow

inventing the outside living

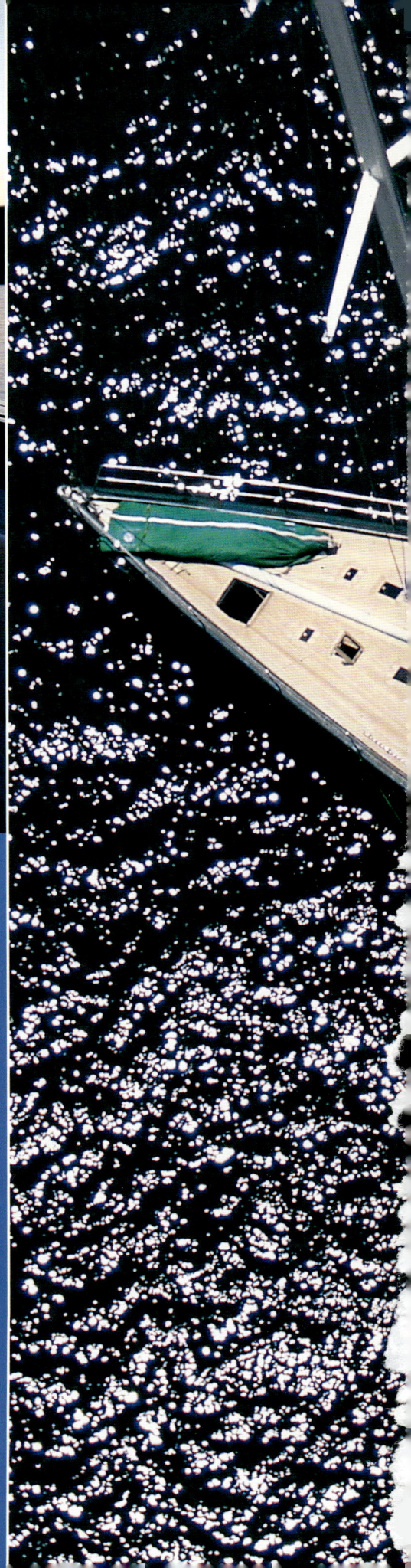

Teak-laid decks are designed around the outdoor sailing lifestyle with several and safe social areas for dining, sunbathing and relaxing.

WallyPower yachts feature forward guest areas with extra privacy and cooling breezes for sunning and dining.

unique and inimitable

"Satisfaction. More than Imitation," advertising campaign 1999

Wally is more than the sum of its parts.

WALLY'S BESPOKE SOLUTIONS ARE UNIQUE TO THEIR PRODUCTS.
THE DESIGN PROCESS INVOLVES STRATEGIC CREATIVE
THINKING TO DEVELOP INTEGRATED SOLUTIONS ON MANY
DIFFERENT LEVELS THAT ARE IMPOSSIBLE TO COPY.

racing a cruiser

OWNING A WALLY INCLUDES MEMBERSHIP OF THE MOST EXCLUSIVE

YACHT CLUB IN THE WORLD, THE WALLY CLASS, WITH RACING IN MAJOR

INTERNATIONAL REGATTAS AT GLAMOROUS VENUES.

The Wally designs cross the boundary between cruising and racing yachts and so are not constrained by any existing rating rules.

"For our summer holiday of 2005 I took my family on board
our Wally 94 Y3K and we cruised the western Mediterranean
in style and comfort. Only two weeks later, after changing
the boat in just a few hours from cruising into racing mode,
we took part in the prestigious Maxi Yacht Rolex Cup
off Porto Cervo, Sardinia.

In most demanding wind and weather conditions Y3K not only
won the Wally Class competition but also beat the fleet
of more than forty international maxi yachts on handicap,
among them many flat out racing machines.

This is what Wally-sailing is all about for me: a fast,
comfortable and easy to handle sailing yacht built
in state-of-the-art carbon fibre and titanium materials to
a breathtakingly minimalist design. A unique design of boat
that stuns by its shear beauty, a boat that allows my wife
and children to enjoy living on board and cruising in safety and
a boat that wins ocean races against world class competitors.
The Wally concept and quality is convincing. Subsequently
I have ordered a new Wally yacht with similar lines but slightly
bigger for more space below deck and for even better
performance on the race course. A versatile WallyTender adds
to the pleasure of being part of the Wally family."

Claus-Peter Offen, Y3K

WALLY SET UP THE WALLY DIVISION WITH ITS OWN HANDICAPPING SYSTEM AND CLASS RESULTS SO THAT OWNERS WHO SHARE THE SAME SPIRIT AND VALUES CAN RACE AGAINST EACH OTHER IN CORINTHIAN COMPETITION AND ENJOY SOCIAL ACTIVITIES TOGETHER.

The Wally Class is the largest fleet of yachts over 24 m (80 ft) in the world.

"We take part in events and international regattas
that help us to bind the Wally name with
the exclusiveness of those moments and to show
the competitiveness of our products."
Luca Bassani Antivari

The choice of having Wally build my fourth Gibian was determined by my experience of forty years of international racing competing in offshore events such as the Buenos Aires to Rio race, the Newport to Bermuda, the Admiral's Cup and various Swan regattas in the Mediterranean.

My aim was to dedicate myself to cruising with my family in any part of the world, without sacrificing either performance or comfort, and from time to time participating in a regatta.

My hopes were fulfilled: as soon as Gibian was launched we sailed to Greece and in the years that followed we went to the Azores, cruised the Caribbean islands and participated in Antigua Sailing Week.

During these cruises we experienced some strong emotions, due to atmospheric conditions that were not exactly benign, but I can say that I have never felt so secure in all my years of sailing than I do with Gibian."

Armando Grandi, Gibian

inside out

Introduced on Dangerous but fun,
the wide laminated panoramic
skylight runs all the way forward
from the main companionway hatch
to the mast, flooding the interior
with natural light.

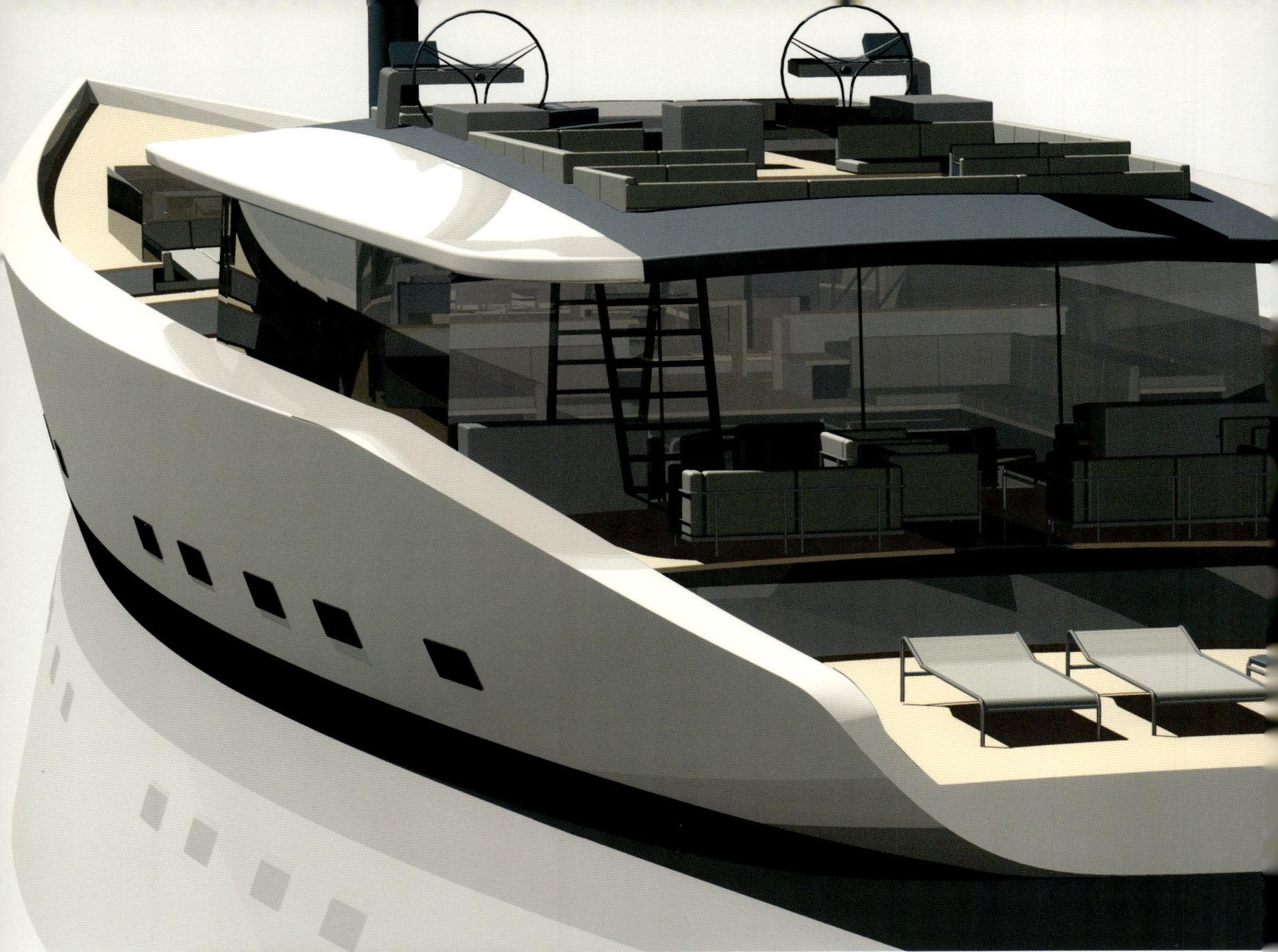

think big

Unconstrained by conventional thinking
and standards, WallyDesign© creates megayachts
that further expand the sailing horizons.

Concepts that are firmly based on sound

engineering and yachting principles,

always putting sailing performance and the life

onboard at the heart of the design.

WIDE OPEN SPACES, UNENCUMBERED PANORAMIC VISTAS,
WALLS OF GLASS AND FLEXIBLE LIVING.

NEW SOLUTIONS, NEW AMBITIONS, NEW EXPERIENCES.

55 m WallyPower

WallyIsland

Pilgrim 80 m

Wally 50 m

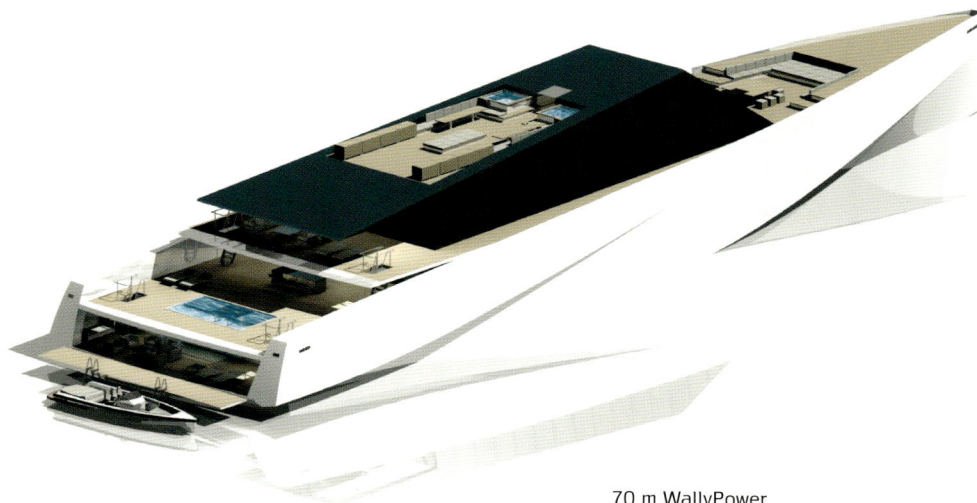
70 m WallyPower

mountain
sailing

Wally applies the same core values of performance and comfort with style to snow skis.

WallySki, the first non-marine product, benefits from the experience of advanced carbon composite construction developed in the shipyards to produce a technically superior ski.

WallySki is 30 per cent lighter than a conventional ski and combines exceptional grip on ice with excellent control in powder resulting in a ski that is extremely easy for beginners as well as responsive for more aggressive skiers.

WallySki is the only fully carbon ski.
Like the yachts, it is highly imitated but remains inimitable
because the form reflects the improved function.

easyrider

The signature
slender vertical bows
on all Wally
yachts, both power
and sail, provide
an easier smoother
ride in rough seas
with virtually
no slamming
or pitching.

The first time I set eyes on a Wally was Tiketitan entering port during Les Voiles de Saint Tropez regatta.

The impression this boat made on me was so great, that I decided, almost immediately, to start sailing again.

After about twenty years of sailing offshore, I had in effect abandoned sailing.

Since then my wife and I spend four or five months a year on a Wally, firstly on the Wally 80 Barong B

and now on board the Wally 94 Barong C.

To analyse the pleasure that these boats bring us, I could say that they evoke:

-beauty of the lines

-speed and vivacity due to their light displacement

-the possibility of having a reduced crew on a relatively large boat.

Naturally, the more that manoeuvring is made easy, the more complex the systems have to be.

To make the most of this type of boat, more than anything you need an excellent skipper gifted with

a sharp sense of maintenance."

Owner Barong C

powering freedom

*PEOPLE SHOULD ENJOY THE FREEDOM
AND BEAUTY OF THE SEA
IN ALL WEATHER CONDITIONS
AND NOT JUST FILL UP THE
MARINAS WITH MORE PARKED BOATS.*

The WallyPower range are designed with a deep-V forebody and vertical bow allowing the boat to cut through the waves with little or no initial pitching motion for a smoother ride.

THE WALLYPOWER DESIGNS
ARE VERY RADICAL IN STYLING.

The WallyPower range demonstrates
extreme functionality and linearity
in exterior styling and interior layout.

**THE FOREDECK IS A MASTER STOKE AS IT IS
COMPLETELY HIDDEN FROM INQUISITIVE EYES.**

open pleasure

THE WALLYTENDER IS A PURE EXPRESSION OF THE
ENJOYMENT OF LIFE ON THE WATER.

THE FAST RUNABOUT IS A GREAT FAMILY BOAT;
WITH SINGLE-LEVEL NON-SLIP TEAK DECK, DEEP
SECURE BULWARKS WITH INTEGRAL HANDRAILS
AND A WALK-AROUND AFT SUNBED.

"Aerodynamic like a jet, Fast as a racing car,
Beautiful like designer furniture."

Giancarlo Giammetti, WallyTender GG

The custom wrap aroun

soft fender keeps the boat dry and is a practical solution for boarding and docking.

carving the sea

The signature elements of the WallyPower range include solid protective bulwarks, an expanse of wide flush teak decks, glass open-plan superstructures, all-round rubbing strakes dispensing the need for fenders and forward sunning and dining areas protected by the deep bulwarks.

Open and airy interiors, almost industrial in design with no false panelling to hide the exposed carbon of the structure, celebrate the advanced construction rather than cover it up.

Glass superstructures enhance the Wally outside-inside living concept. Filters screen the heat and UV rays of the sun with a special double-glazing system.

Water jet propulsion

provides better

manoeuvrability with

the ability to "hover"

in the same place

and turn in a circle

with the vectored thrust.

Water jets give shallower draft and remove the possibility of propeller damage.

smooth operator

The innovative interceptor system on all the WallyPower range allows efficient control of the dynamic trim producing a 30 per cent reduction in resistance when achieving planning speeds.

The interceptor offers faster and smoother acceleration and reduced fuel consumption.

"Thank you Wally for realizing the boat that we desired."

Owner Lunch Boat

the world of interiors

Bright and airy interior spaces
with refreshing contemporary
designs integrate with the sleek
exterior styling.

On some of the projects Wally
work with world-renowned
designers to produce modern
light interiors celebrating
the structural components.

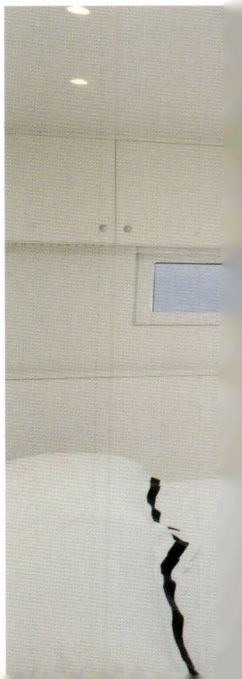

silent running

The Chine Dumper, a patented
Wally feature first used
on the 70 WallyPower, reduces
the noise from slamming
into waves underway and
at anchor, further improving
the quality of the onboard
experience.

letting the outside in

The prism-like glass deckhouses
on the WallyPower designs fully exploit the
inside-outside lifestyle concept introduced
with the "terrace-on-the-sea."

Interior spaces merge easily with the outdoor
deck increasing the living areas
and the laminated glass superstructure
with special UV filters allows 360-degree
views of the seascape.

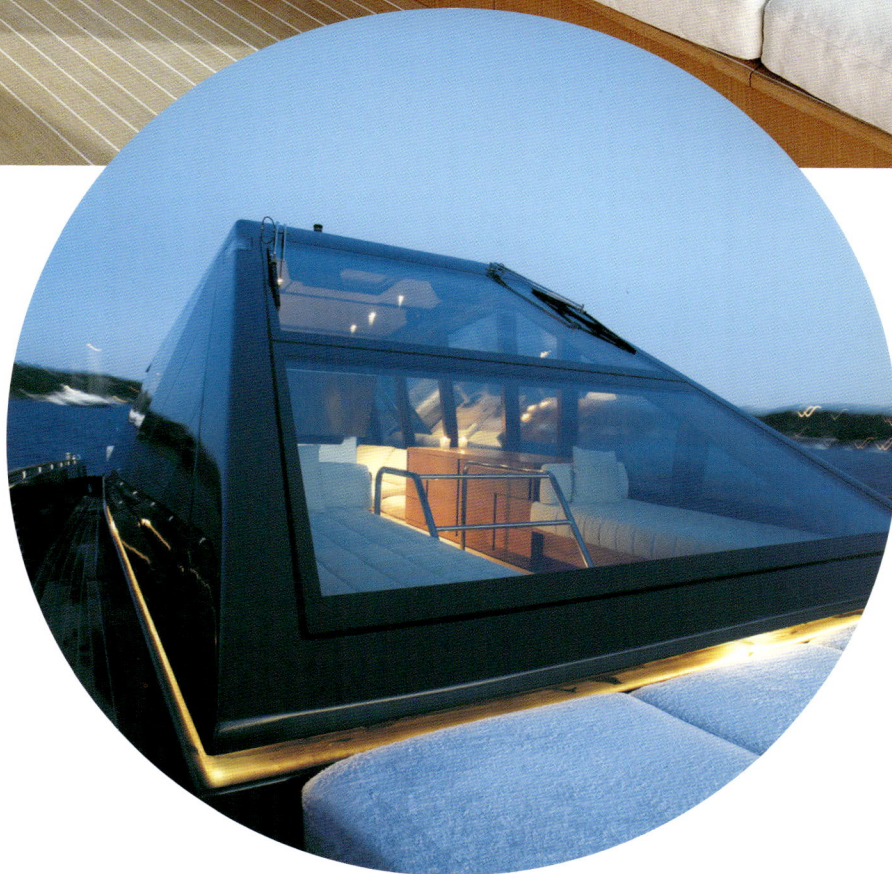

"When you're outside the boat it looks very, very aggressive, almost naughty. But once you get onboard you immediately have a feeling of peace and tranquility. Everyone is surprised by this."   Luca Bassani Antivari

Assertive looks and 60-knot-plus triple gas turbine power has made the 118 WallyPower a worldwide celebrity.

The dramatic statement of the angular and purposeful aerodynamic shape of the 118 WallyPower shows itself in the highlights and shadows of the single tone colour scheme. Air intakes of a jet fighter and angular superstructure very reminiscent of a stealth bomber.

At anchor the ultra-wide boarding and swimming platform is extended aft and the side bulwarks drop down to enlarge the view from the saloon.

a design icon

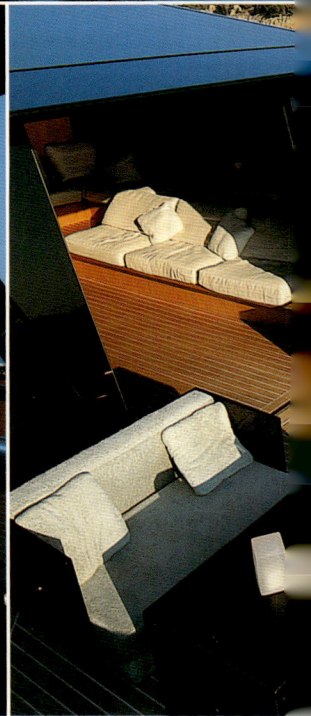

The 118 WallyPower has an amazingly smooth motion at high speed in rough seas, with reduced pitching and deceleration, unheard of in conventional boats of a similar size and displacement.

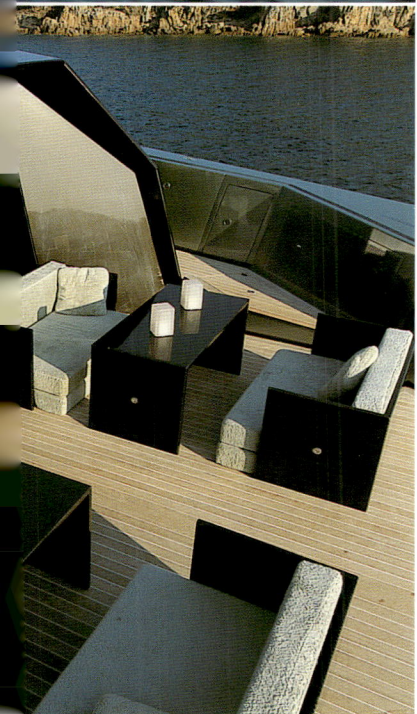

building the brand

Wally is a process of identifying and addressing a need and fulfilling it in the most competent and creative way possible. It has never been a single product, a shipyard or even a design company.

The Wally system is a way of thinking and experimenting how to get the maximum enjoyment out of the precious resource of leisure time.

For me Wally represents a real revolution in the nautical world, both sailing and motor. I love sailing on a Wally because she unites innovation in the lines and the technology with exhilarating performance and simplicity of use. Added to the pleasure of cruising is the fun to be had racing in the Wally Class within the major regattas in the Mediterranean."

Owner Dangerous but fun

The "soul" in Wally is part of the greater plan to build
a new brand of advanced leisure products,
a brand that has core values of technical excellence
and outstanding performance with great style.

THE WALLY BRAND MEANS MAN'S POTENTIAL TO

CHANGE, TO CHALLENGE, TO ENJOY THE NATURAL

ENVIRONMENT WHETHER IT IS SKIING DOWN A

MOUNTAIN, ENJOYING A SWIM OFF THE BACK OF

YOUR YACHT OR CRUISING UNDER THE STARS.

private protection

Deep protective bulwarks and wide side decks on the large Wally sailing yachts are the perfect practical answer for safety and style.

Reminiscent of vintage and classic yachts, the bulwarks remove the need for lifelines and stanchions, leaving just the pure clean line of the matching paint of the bulwark to merge into the hull and superstructure.

The second Wallygator
(now Nariida) is launched,
the 32 m (105 ft) ketch
is the first "Wally revolution."
The first large yacht built in
advanced composites with
push button hydraulic sail
trimming and the concealed
Wally remote-controlled
underwater anchor system.

The first two Wallys are
delivered to clients:
the 24 m (80 ft)
Magic Carpet and Kauris II.

1994

1995

1997

1998

Tiketitan is launched,
the 27 m (88 ft) sloop is
the third "Wally revolution"
with canting keel,
terrace-on-the-sea
and in-boom furling 3DL fully
battened mainsail.

Genie of the Lamp
is launched, a 24 m
(80 ft) sloop that
can be handled by
just one person:
the second
"Wally revolution."

The Wally Class is born:
Wallys participate in racing
events with their own class
results and class rules.

wally milestones

The first 25 m (83 ft) Wallygator (now Mr. Gecko) is launched with carbon mast and swept back spreaders, flush deck with separate cockpits for technical and social use, sheets running under the deck, interior layout with master cabin forward.

1989   **1991**   **1993**

Wally is founded.

Luca Bassani Antivari, President and founder of Wally, decides to build his own family yacht combining the comfort and luxury of a large cruiser with the performance of a maxi racer, making sailing safer and easier.

The 118 WallyPower is delivered.

The first units of the new
70 WallyPower
and 47 WallyPower models
are launched.

2003

2004

2005

2006

The WallyDesign©
department is created,
dedicated to the design
and styling
of megayacht projects.

Alexia is launched,
the 30 m (100 ft) sloop
is the first large cruiser
with water ballast
technology.

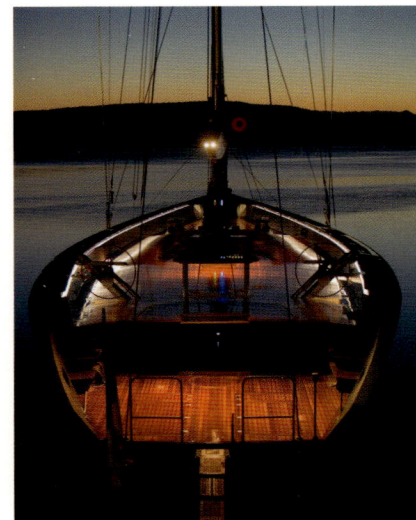

Esence is launched,
the 44 m (143 ft)
supersloop
is the fourth
"Wally revolution"
with raised bulwarks.

Wally sponsors and promotes
two new sailing speed records:
one from Saint Tropez to Monaco,
and one from Monaco to Porto Cervo.

WALLY
R E C O R D

Wally enters the motor yacht market.

The first WallyTender is launched.

1999   **2000**   **2001**   **2002**

Carrera is launched, a 24 m
(80 ft) sloop featuring the
innovative Wally lifting keel.

Wally launches the WallySki.

Wally sets up WMagic, a new
boatyard in Tunisia,
specialising in the highest
technology construction of
advanced composite yachts.

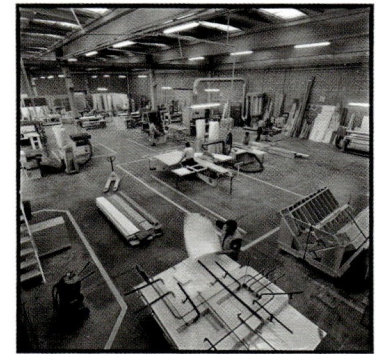

Wally sets up the WallyEurope
shipyards.

Magic Carpet² is launched,
the 29 m (94 ft) sloop
is the first yacht to feature
the Wally high performance
lifting keel with trim tab.

The uniqueness of Wally products is achieved
by building technical innovation
into the very heart of the manufacturing process.
The Wally brand is always evolving.

"We will always keep our soul as a company

that always brings something new

and functional to the market.

We never consider the adventure, the design

experience, as being over."

Luca Bassani Antivari

"Wally, and your heart is set on fire."

Carlo Sama, Tango

catalogue

SAIL

yacht	type	designer	builder	year
Esense	143' sloop	Bill Tripp Design/Wally	WallyEurope, Italy	2006
Shaka	80' sloop	Farr Yacht Design/Wally	WallyEurope, Italy	2006
Tango	80' sloop	Farr Yacht Design/Wally	WallyEurope, Italy	2006
Barong C	94' sloop	German Frers/Wally	WallyEurope, Italy	2005
Open Season	94' sloop	German Frers/Wally	WallyEurope, Italy	2005
Aori	80' sloop	Farr Yacht Design/Wally	WallyEurope, Italy	2004
Indio	80' sloop	Farr Yacht Design/Wally	WallyEurope, Italy	2004
Alexia	100' sloop	Javier Soto Acebal/Wally	WallyEurope, Italy	2004
Dangerous but fun	80' sloop	Farr Yacht Design/Wally	WallyEurope, Italy	2004
Y3K	94' sloop	German Frers/Wally	WallyEurope, Italy	2003
Wallyño	60' sloop	Farr Yacht Design/Wally	Carroll Marine, USA	2002
Magic Carpet²	94' sloop	German Frers/Wally	WallyEurope, Italy	2002
Dark Shadow	100' sloop	German Frers/Wally	WallyEurope, Italy	2002
Kauris III	107' sloop	German Frers/Wally	WallyEurope, Italy	2002
Tiketitoo	88' sloop	German Frers/Wally	CNB, Italy	2001
Carrera	80' sloop	German Frers/Wally	CNB, Italy	2000
Barong B	80' sloop	German Frers/Wally	CNB, Italy	2000
Gibian	100' sloop	German Frers/Wally	CNB, Italy	2000
Tuamata	80' sloop	German Frers/Wally	CNB, Italy	2000
Kenora	107' sloop	Luca Brenta & Co./Wally	Pendennis Shipyard, UK	1999
Askherout	80' sloop	German Frers/Wally	CNB, Italy	1999
Yam	95' sloop	German Frers/Wally	CNB, Italy	1999
Tiketitan	88' sloop	German Frers/Wally	Green Marine, UK	1998
Itaca	67' sloop	German Frers/Wally	CNB, Italy	1998
Wally 'B'	107' sloop	Luca Brenta & Co./Wally	Pendennis Shipyard, UK	1998
Ippogrifo II	80' sloop	German Frers/Wally	Camper & Nicholsons, UK	1997
J One	80' sloop	German Frers/Wally	CNB, Italy	1997

yacht	type		designer	builder	year
Genie of the Lamp	80'	sloop	German Frers/Wally	Maxi Dolphin, Italy	1995
Nariida	105'	ketch	Luca Brenta & Co./Wally	Concordia Custom Yachts, USA	1994
Edimetra	65'	sloop	German Frers	Yachting Development, NZ	1994
Good Job Guys	60'	sloop	Luca Brenta & Co.	Yachting Development, NZ	1993
Mr. Gecko	83'	sloop	Luca Brenta & Co.	Sangermani, Italy	1991

POWER

yacht	type		designer	builder	year
118 WallyPower	118'	fast motoryacht	Wally/Intermarine	Intermarine, Italy	2003
70 WallyPower open	70'	motoryacht	Wally/Allseas	WallyEurope, Italy	2006
Nounouche	70'	motoryacht	Wally/Allseas	WallyEurope, Italy	2006
Lunch Boat	70'	motoryacht	Wally/Allseas	WallyEurope, Italy	2005
47 WallyPower	47'	motor boat	Wally/Allseas	WMagic, Tunisia	2005
WallyTender overnight cruiser	45'	motor boat	Wally/Allseas	WMagic, Tunisia	2002
WallyTender day cruiser	45'	motor boat	Wally/Allseas	WMagic, Tunisia	2001
WallyDinghy	33'	motor boat	Wally/Allseas	WallyEurope, Italy	2004

SKI

type	year
Minipowder	2006
FreeWally	2006
WallyPowder	2004
Wallyño	2004
Magic	2002
Freeride	2001
Traditional	2001
Original	2000

esense

year	2006
length o.a.	43.70 m – 143' 4"
displacement	140 tons – 308,647 lbs
accommodation	8 guests – 6 crew

shaka

year	2006
length o.a.	24.00 m – 80'
displacement	33 tons – 73.920 lbs
accommodation	6 guests – 2 crew

tango

year	2006
length o.a.	24.00 m – 80'
displacement	33 tons – 73.920 lbs
accommodation	6+2 guests – 2 crew
race victories	Zegna Trophy 2006 Wally Division

barong c

year	2005
length o.a.	28.55 m – 93' 8"
displacement	45 tons – 98,208 lbs
accommodation	4 guests – 4 crew

open season

year	2005
length o.a.	28.71 m – 94'2"
displacement	42 tons – 92,594 lbs
accommodation	6+2 guests – 2+2 crew

aori

year	2004
length o.a.	24.00 m – 80'
displacement	33 tons – 73,920 lbs
accommodation	6+2 guests – 2 crew

indio

year	2004
length o.a.	24.00 m – 80'
displacement	35 tons – 77,162 lbs
accommodation	6+1 guests – 2 crew

alexia

year	2004
length o.a.	30.63 m – 100'4"
displacement	49 tons – 108,026 lbs
accommodation	6 guests – 4 crew
race victories	Maxi Yacht Rolex Cup 2004 Wally Division
	Les Voiles de Saint Tropez 2004 Wally Division
	Les Voiles de Saint Tropez 2005 Wally Division

dangerous but fun

year	2004
length o.a.	24.00 m – 80'
displacement	33 tons – 73,920 lbs
accommodation	6+2 guests – 2 crew

y3k

year	2003
length o.a.	28.55 m – 93' 8"
displacement	42.5 tons – 93,696 lbs
accommodation	6+3 guests – 2 crew
race victories	Palmavela 2004
	Zegna Trophy 2004 Wally Division
	Giraglia Rolex Cup 2004 Wally Division
	Palmavela Hublot Regatta 2005 IRC and Wally Divisions
	Maxi Yacht Rolex Cup 2005 Wally Division
	Wally Class 2005 Hublot Trophy
	Hublot Palmavela 2006 Wally Division
awards	Superyacht Design Award 2003: Best Sailing Yacht under 36 metres

wallyño

year	2003
length o.a.	18.46 m – 60' 6"
displacement	15.5 tons – 34,171 lbs
accommodation	6 guests
race victories	Zegna Trophy 2003
	Zegna Trophy 2003 Wally Division
	Giraglia Rolex Cup 2003 Wally Division
	Maxi Yacht Rolex Cup 2003 Wally Division
	Les Voiles de Saint Tropez 2003 Overall IRC

magic carpet[2]

year	2002
length o.a.	28.55 m – 93' 8"
displacement	32 tons – 70,547 lbs
accommodation	6+1 guests – 2+2 crew
race victories	Zegna Trophy 2005 Wally Division
	Maxi Yacht Rolex Cup 2006 Wally Division
	Les Voiles de Saint Tropez 2006 Wally Division

dark shadow

year	2002
length o.a.	30.45 m – 100'
displacement	64 tons – 141,280 lbs
accommodation	6 guests - 4 crew
race victories	Giraglia Rolex Cup 2006 Wally Division

kauris III

year	2002
length o.a.	32.83 m – 107' 8"
displacement	67 tons – 147,710 lbs
accommodation	6 guests – 4 crew
race victories	Pirelli Trophy 2003
	Pirelli Trophy 2004

tiketitoo

year	2001
length o.a.	27.00 m – 88' 7"
displacement	32 tons – 70,547 lbs
accommodation	6 guests – 2 crew
awards	ADI – Industrial Design Association Compasso d'Oro 2004
	ShowBoats International Award 2001: Most Innovative Sailing Yacht

carrera

year	2000
length o.a.	24.00 m – 80'
displacement	32 tons – 70,548 lbs
accommodation	6 guests – 2 crew

race victories

vae victis	Maxi Yacht Rolex Cup 2001 Wally Division
carrera	Les Voiles de Saint Tropez 2002 Wally Division

barong b

year	2000
length o.a.	24.00 m – 80'
displacement	33 tons – 72,753 lbs
accommodation	6 guests – 2 crew

gibian

year	2000
length o.a.	30.45 m – 100'
displacement	68 tons –149,914 lbs
accommodation	6+2 guests – 4 crew

tuamata

year	2000
length o.a.	24.00 m – 80'
displacement	35 tons – 77,161 lbs
accommodation	6 guests – 2 crew

kenora

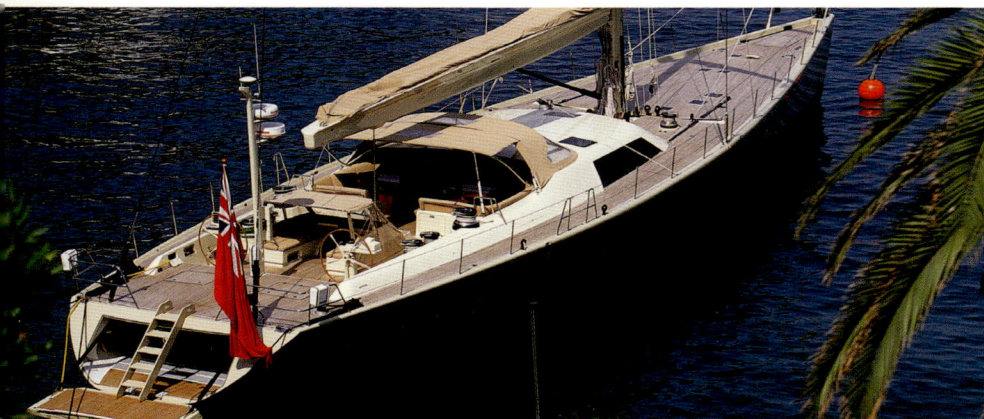

year	1999
length o.a.	32.72 m – 107'4"
displacement	85 tons – 187,393 lbs
accommodation	6 guests – 4 crew
awards	Superyacht Design Award 1999: Best Sailing Yacht under 36 metres

askheruout

year	1999
length o.a.	24.00 m – 80'
displacement	31.5 tons – 69,445 lbs
accommodation	6+1 guests – 2 crew

yam

year	1999
length o.a.	29.30 m – 96'1"
displacement	60 tons – 132,277 lbs
accommodation	6+1 guests – 4 crew
race victories	Maxi Yacht Rolex Cup 1999 Over Hundred Division ICAYA

tiketitan

year	1998
length o.a.	27.00 m – 88' 7"
displacement	32 tons – 70,547 lbs
accommodation	6 guests – 2 crew
race victories	Maxi Yacht Rolex Cup 2000 Bentley Trophy
	Giraglia Rolex Cup 2001 Wally Division
	Giraglia Rolex Cup 2005 Wally Division

itaca

year	1998
length o.a.	20.55 m – 67'5"
displacement	22 tons – 48,500 lbs
accommodation	4 guests – 2 crew
race victories annica	Les Voiles de Saint Tropez 2003 Wally Division

wally b

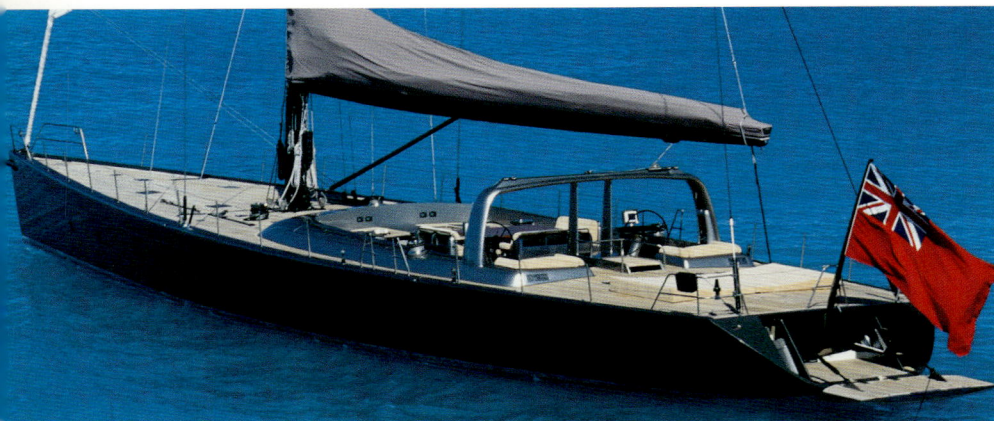

year	1998
length o.a.	32.72 m –107' 4"
displacement	75.4 tons – 166.228 lbs
accommodation	6 guests – 4 crew
awards	Superyacht Design Award 1998: Best Sailing Yacht under 36 metres
	ShowBoats International Award 1998: Best Sailing Yacht under 38 metres

ippogrifo II

year	1997
length o.a.	24.00 m – 80'
displacement	35 tons – 77,162 lbs
accommodation	6 guests – 3 crew
race victories kauris II	Zegna Trophy 2002 Wally Division

j one

year	1997
length o.a.	24.00 m – 80'
displacement	31.5 tons – 69,445 lbs
accommodation	6+1 guests – 2 crew

race victories
magic carpet

Zegna Trophy 1999 Wally Division
Giraglia Rolex Cup 1999 Wally Division
Les Voiles de Saint Tropez 1999 Wally Division
Zegna Trophy 2000 Wally Division
Giraglia Rolex Cup 2000 Wally Division
Maxi Yacht Rolex Cup 2000 Cruising Light Division
Zegna Trophy 2001 Wally Division
Les Voiles de Saint Tropez 2001 Wally Division
Giraglia Rolex Cup 2002 Wally Division
Maxi Yacht Rolex Cup 2002 Wally Division

genie of the lamp

year	1995
length o.a.	24.00 m – 80'
displacement	27 tons – 59,525 lbs
accommodation	6+1 guests – 2 crew

race victories	Maxi Yacht Rolex Cup 1999 Cruising Division
	Maxi Yacht Rolex Cup 1999 Wally Division

nariida

year	1994
length o.a.	32.04 m – 105'
displacement	60 tons – 132,660 lbs
accommodation	8+3 guests – 4 crew

race victories	
wallygator	ShowBoats Cup 1997, Giraglia Race 1997 First to finish
nariida	Les Voiles de Saint Tropez 2000 Wally Division
	Wally Speed Record Monaco-Saint Tropez 45 nm - 3 hours, 4 minutes and 40 seconds average speed: 15 kts 20 October1999
	World Sailing Speed Record Monaco-Porto Cervo 195 nm - 15 hours 24 minutes and 59 seconds average speed: 12.64 kts 5-6 October 2003
award	
wallygator	ShowBoats International Award 1994: Most Innovative Sailing Yacht

edimetra VI

year	1994
length o.a.	20.05 m – 65' 78"
displacement	23.5 tons – 51,807 lbs
accommodation	6 guests – 2 crew

race victories	
rrose sèlavy	Nioulargue 1994 Overall, Zegna Trophy 2005, Maxi Yacht Rolex Cup 1995, Antigua Sailing Week 1996 Maxi Division, Maxi Yacht Rolex Cup 1996, Zegna Trophy 2007 IMS Division
edimetra VI	Pirelli Trophy 2006 Overall, Zegna Trophy 2006, Zegna Trophy 2006 IMS Division, Giraglia Rolex Cup 2006 Maxi Division, Giraglia Rolex Cup 2005 Maxi Division, Pirelli Trophy 2004 Maxi Division, Maxi Yacht Rolex Cup 2001 IMS Division, Tre Golfi Regatta 2000 Città di Napoli Cup Overall, Giraglia Rolex Cup 1999 Overall

good job boys

year	1993
length o.a.	18.28 m – 60'
displacement	18 tons – 39,683 lbs
accommodation	4+2 guests – 2 crew
race victories	Pirelli Trophy 2000

mr. gecko

year	1991
length o.a.	25.30 m – 83'
displacement	33 tons – 73,920 lbs
accommodation	6 guests – 4 crew

118 wallypower

year	2003
length o.a.	36.00 – 118'
engine	3 x DDC TF50 gas turbines + 2 x Cummins 370 max power 16,800 Hp + 740 Hp
accommodation	6 guests – 6 crew
max speed	63 knots
awards	2005 featured in the movie *The Island*, produced by DreamWorks and directed by Michael Bay
	2004 only boat selected by the San Francisco Museum of Modern Art for the major architecture and design exhibition "Glamour: Fabricating affluence"
	Millennium Yacht Design Award (MYDA): a design that remarkably contributed to the development of the concept of the yacht layout

nounouche

year	2006
length o.a.	21.90 m – 72'
engine	2 x MTU 10V 2000 M93, max power 3,040 Hp
accommodation	3+1 guests – 2 crew
max speed	45 knots

70 wallypower open

year	2006
length o.a.	21.90 m - 72'
engine	2 x MTU 10V 2000 M93, max power 3,040 Hp
accommodation	2 guests – 2 crew
max speed	47.5 knots

lunch boat

year	2005
length o.a.	21.90 m – 72'
engine	2 x MTU 10V 2000 M93, max power 3,040 Hp
accommodation	3+1 guests – 2 crew
max speed	45 knots

47 wallypower

year	2005
length o.a.	14.70 m – 48' 2"
engine	2 x Yanmar 6LY2A-STP, max power 880 Hp
accommodation	2 guests – 1 crew
max speed	35 knots

wallytender day cruiser

year	2001
length o.a.	13.60 m – 45'
diesel package	2 x Cummins-Mercruiser D4.2L max power 640 Hp
max speed	40 knots
petrol package	2 x Mercruiser 496 MAG HO DTS max power 840 Hp
max speed	50 knots

wallytender overnight cruiser

year	2002
length o.a.	13.60 m – 45'
diesel package	2 x Cummins-Mercruiser D4.2L max power 640 Hp
accommodation	2 guests
max speed	40 knots
petrol package	2 x Mercruiser 496 MAG HO DTS max power 840 Hp
max speed	50 knots

wallydinghy

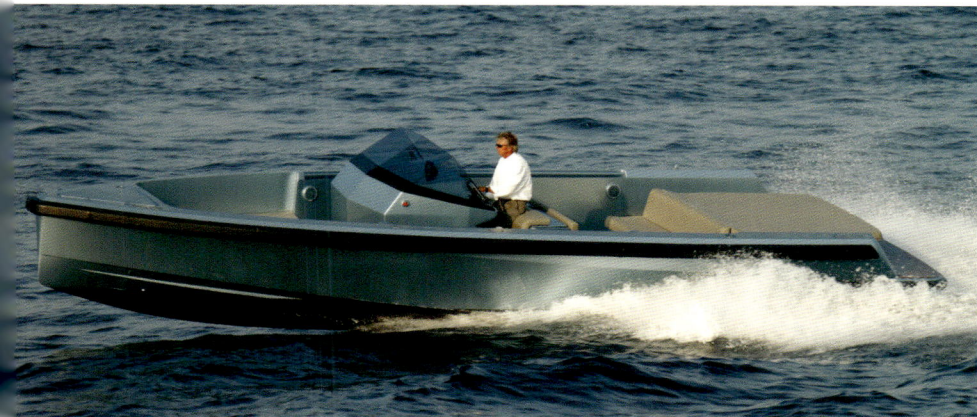

year	2004
length o.a.	9.99 m – 32' 9"
engine	2 x Mercruiser 2.8L, max power 400 Hp
max speed	38 knots

original

year 2000

Developed to be a truly
all-round ski, suitable
for ice as well
as for powder, designed
more for carving turns
than for traditional
slalom skiing.

Built using sandwich
technology in carbon
fibre with wood core.

tradition

year 2001

Dedicated to those
who are less inclined
to the new carving style,
narrower than
the Original.

Built using sandwich
technology in carbon
fibre with wood core.

freeride

year 2001

Developed specifically
for the Freeride style of skiing.

Built using sandwich
technology in carbon fibre
with wood core.

magic

year 2002

Developed with the
same target as the
Original, but with a
shape that makes it
more agile.

Built using advanced
composite technology
in carbon fibre with
wood core and
postcured in an
autoclave.

wallyño

year 2004

Short and very agile, developed for the slalom style.

Built using sandwich technology in carbon fibre with wood core.

wallypowder

year 2004

The first ski in the world developed specifically for off piste, it allows beginners to easily deal with powder snow conditions. For the expert skier it handles powder like a snowboard, both in slalom and carving styles with large curves offering the possibility to ski at any speed. Thanks to the advanced composite construction, it is much lighter, easier and more precise than the FatBoy skis developed in Canada for off piste.

Built using advanced composite technology in carbon fibre with wood core and postcured in an autoclave.

freewally

year 2006

Developed from the shape of the Original model in order to have the same all-round characteristics, but with a raised tail to also satisfy the requirements of enthusiasts for Freeride style skiing and constructed in advanced composites to make it even more responsive and aggressive.

Built using advanced composite technology in carbon fibre with wood core and postcured in an autoclave.

minipowder

year 2006

Like the WallyPowder, this model is specifically for off piste skiing but is slightly shorter and narrower for the less expert powder skier.

Built using advanced composite technology in carbon fibre with wood core and postcured in an autoclave.

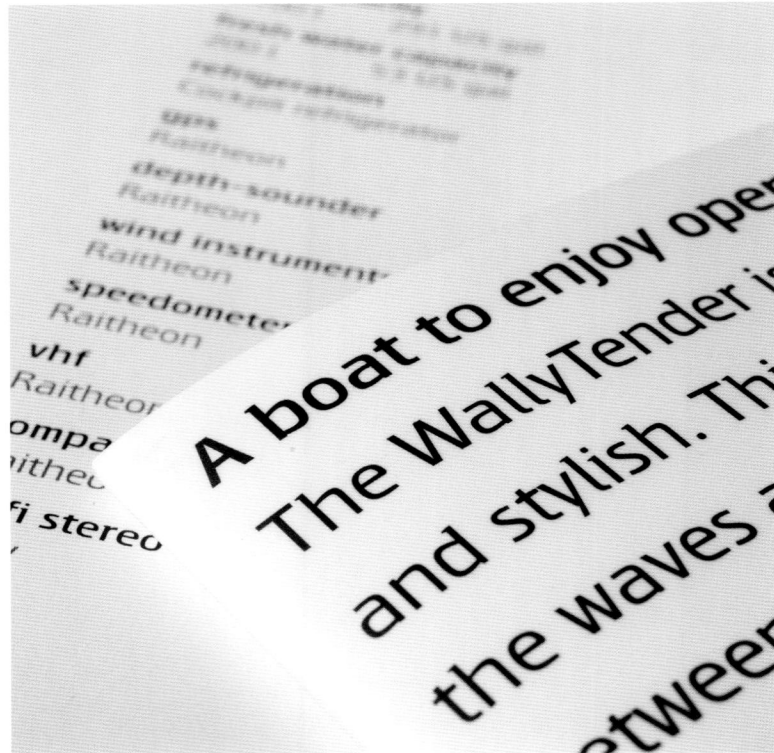

WallyType is a custom font. It served to build the Wally corporate identity and is conceived to go beyond a use limited to logo and product names.

This volume was printed for Mondadori Electa SpA at Verona Mondadori Printing SpA in 2006